"What a joy it has been to read Bryan's firsthand account of treks across Asia and the United States in search of new ways Jesus is being loved and followed. We are introduced to Hindus, Muslims, Buddhists, Native Americans, and American youth experiencing Jesus freed from unhelpful Western trappings and traditions. What we find here are real-life narratives skillfully shared in a relaxed, unhurried manner, allowing the reader to enter into the author's experience and reflect with him on what he sees. I find this book inspiring and full of hope. I highly recommend it to anyone asking hard questions about how Jesus can be introduced in ways that make him accessible to the peoples of the world who have often tragically felt he is off-limits for them."

John J. Travis, PhD, missiologist, affiliate faculty, Fuller Theological Seminary

"With a journalist's observant eye, Bryan Bishop spent years traveling the world to report with engaging detail about people who meet to worship Jesus. What makes *Boundless* riveting is that these followers of Jesus were born as Hindus, Buddhists, Muslims, and tribal peoples—and to Western eyes, their forms of worship will be unfamiliar, even strange. Throughout his journeys, Bishop relentlessly asks similar questions: In a world where the word *Christian* has been filled with all kinds of nonbiblical meanings, could we simply invite people to follow Jesus but not use the word? What do these Hindu/Buddhist/Muslim/tribal followers of Jesus *actually* believe about Jesus? Read *Boundless* to see what church looks like among peoples who haven't been told to check their ethnicity at the door."

EJ Martin, editor, *Where There Was No Church: Postcards from Followers of Jesus in the Muslim World*

"Bryan Bishop's stimulating accounts of alternate patterns of discipleship to Jesus will instruct and intrigue. His internal dialog invokes the key questions and problems evident in new Jesus movements developing across the globe. Every traveler along a similar path to Bryan's will recount different stories and grapple with different nuances of the challenges of incarnational expressions of biblical faith, but all will appreciate his sensitive and insightful analysis."

H. L. Richard, author, *Rethinking Hindu Ministry*

BOUNDLESS

WHAT GLOBAL EXPRESSIONS OF FAITH
TEACH US ABOUT FOLLOWING JESUS

BRYAN BISHOP

BakerBooks

a division of Baker Publishing Group
Grand Rapids, Michigan

Published by Baker Books
a division of Baker Publishing Group
P.O. Box 6287, Grand Rapids, MI 49516-6287
www.bakerbooks.com

Printed in the United States of America

Library of Congress Cataloging-in-Publication Data is on file at the Library of Congress, Washington, DC.

ISBN 978-0-8010-1716-2

Author is represented by WordServe Literary, Inc., www.wordserveliterary.com

15   16   17   18   19   20   21   7   6   5   4   3   2   1

Contents

To my parents,
Clarence and Theresa Bishop

1

The Man in the Beginning

The man in the center of the storm looked surprisingly ordinary when I finally met him. I encountered him in a large resort in Thailand. I'd come there for a conference called "Mercy Ministries, Frontier Mission, and Urban Mission."

On the first day, when our morning lecture ended, I looked around the table at the five people who had been taking notes with me. I caught the eye of the man sitting to my left. He had brown hair, bangs, and a goatee. I said hello. He smiled, shook my hand, and introduced himself. I found out he was from Australia, and worked in an Asian country that is predominantly Muslim. He spoke quietly and slowly.

"It's quite a remarkable story, actually," he said.

He started telling me about a Muslim man who had a vision of Jesus, without any contact from Christians. As soon as he said that, I knew I'd heard the rest of the story. I realized, this is the guy! I couldn't believe I was sitting right next to him.

I had heard about Randy several months before this meeting.[1] He and I work for the same organization, Youth With A Mission, also known as YWAM. We both had joined a YWAM email discussion forum that included hundreds of participants. On this forum I had seen an email from Randy that gave a few tantalizing details about his work.

The story began with a Muslim man who one day had a vision of Jesus. I'll call this man Ibrahim. What Ibrahim saw that day powerfully changed his views. He encountered the man the Qur'an refers to as *Isa al-Masih*, Jesus the Messiah. In the vision, Jesus revealed His true nature to Ibrahim, who then saw Jesus not simply as a prophet but as the living God, his Savior. He began to read the Bible and started telling his friends and family what had happened to him. Some of them started to believe as well. In less than a year the group of Jesus-followers grew to fifty. During this whole time, they had no contact with Christians.

Even after Ibrahim and the other Jesus-followers understood that Jesus was their Savior, they still viewed themselves as Muslims. Many became more faithful in their daily prayers. Now they bowed down to thank God for their salvation in Jesus. The males who had attended the mosque continued to do so, and the believers in Jesus also met weekly on their own to study the Bible. They lived out their faith entirely within the Muslim community.

A Christian man working in this area met Ibrahim. After hearing Ibrahim's story, the Christian offered to help Ibrahim learn how to study the Bible. The Christian, though, did not ask Ibrahim to become a Christian. He simply supported Ibrahim and the others as they followed Jesus as Muslims. He made no attempt to encourage these people to call themselves Christians. This Christian man was Randy, the man I met in Thailand.

As this network of Muslim believers in Jesus grew in number, they came to the attention of a Christian group nearby. The fact that Ibrahim and the others still maintained their mosque attendance, still did their daily prayers, and still called themselves Muslims alarmed the Christian group. These Christians wanted to teach the Muslim believers how to follow Christian teaching properly.

They sought out many of the members of Ibrahim's network and convinced them to come to a three-month Bible training program. One day, they took half of the group to a place many hours' journey away. This caused great distress among those who remained behind, who didn't know where their family members and friends had gone. Randy also was very upset.

When the Bible training program was over, most of the participants returned. They all called themselves Christians now and no longer participated in their former Muslim activities. Their family and friends rejected them. The movement that had been spreading so rapidly through Ibrahim and his network now slowed.

Randy continued to work with Ibrahim. When Randy wrote his email, he and his teammates were just beginning to see the group start to grow again.

When I read Randy's email, I was fascinated. At least three things intrigued me. First, Ibrahim and his friends came to faith without any contact with Christians. What was this vision like that had such a powerful effect on Ibrahim? Second, this Christian man, Randy, didn't tell these Muslims to call themselves Christians. He left them as Muslims. He even encouraged them to stay in their Muslim community. Why would he do that? And third, the biggest opposition to these new believers came not from the Muslim imams or from the government but from the Christian community!

The whole story raised so many questions. Was Randy's approach biblical? Aren't there Muslim beliefs that are incompatible with biblical faith? Could this kind of approach be used elsewhere? And what do these Muslim believers in Jesus actually believe?

Now, on this April morning in 1998, I realized I had Randy sitting right in front of me. I had to resist the urge to ask Randy to please skip the rest of the conference and just answer my questions. But I did ask him to have lunch with me, and he agreed. And then after lunch, we continued to talk in the empty restaurant through the whole afternoon as the next lecture went on without us. For the rest of the week, we skipped session after session as I followed Randy through the sliding doors that automatically opened from one part of the complex to another. We walked through the seventeen-story atrium with its glass elevators and greenery. We sat in lounges and cafés and stood in wood-paneled hallways. And Randy patiently answered many of my questions.

Growth of a Movement

I asked Randy if he knew of any other cases of people from an Islamic background following Jesus but still calling themselves Muslims. Were other people using Randy's approach, and where did it come from? Randy admitted he had only limited knowledge of the bigger picture. In early 1998 there was very little information available on anyone doing this kind of work. In the Muslim country where he lived, Randy said two men had helped to pioneer this approach. They both worked with an organization that Randy named, which was a conservative evangelical group known for its emphasis on Bible study and memorization. I was quite surprised to hear that two of their members were involved with such an extreme method.

In the years since my first talk with Randy, the approach he described to me has grown into many movements in many parts of the globe. It has become a hotly debated subject in many parts of the missionary community. Outside of those circles, though, most people still don't know about it.

In 2001 the Center for the Study of Global Christianity, one of the most respected mission research organizations, gave an idea of just how widespread this phenomenon is. They reported, "14 million converted Hindus, Buddhists, and Muslims have opted to remain within those religions in order to witness for Christ as active believers in Jesus as Lord."[2]

In other words, these fourteen million people have chosen to follow Jesus, but they haven't decided to become Christians. They don't call themselves Christians and don't attend Christian churches. They follow Jesus as Lord but stay within their Hindu, Buddhist, or Muslim religious culture.

Some call themselves Muslim Followers of Jesus. Some call themselves *Yeshu Bhaktas*, or Hindu Followers of Jesus. Some Buddhists use the term "Children of God" to describe their faith in Jesus.

Sometimes these Christ-followers have been called "insiders," because they have chosen to stay inside their own culture, including their religious culture, to live out their faith.

Theological studies done on several of these groups have shown that the majority of them believe the core theological tenants of the Bible. They believe in God the Father, the divinity of Jesus, the saving work of Jesus, the indwelling of the Spirit, and the inspiration of the Scriptures.

In spite of these findings, though, for many people the approach Randy described to me raises a whole lot of questions, the same kinds of questions that first entered my mind.

I asked Randy, "So these people call themselves Muslims?"

"Yes," he said.

"What do they believe about Jesus?"

"They believe Jesus is God, that He died for their sins, and that it's no longer they who live but Jesus who lives in them."

I was fishing around now through what I knew of Muslims. I wondered what the practices of these Muslim believers in Christ might be. Would they still follow the Five Pillars of Islam: the confession that there is no God but Allah and Muhammad is Allah's messenger, the prayers five times a day, the fasting during daylight hours of the month of Ramadan, the giving of alms, and the pilgrimage to Mecca? I asked about the easy ones first.

"Do they still pray five times a day?"

"They are often more dedicated in doing the prayers than they were before," Randy said. "Before the evening prayers, they meet together as believers. They plan to start having communion together during this time."

"What about the fast? Do they fast during Ramadan?"

"Yes, they keep the fast. This is a great time of celebration and dedication to God."

Okay, now for the harder question. "What about Muhammad? Do they say the confession that there is no deity but Allah and Muhammad is Allah's messenger?"

Randy admitted that the Islamic confession poses a crucial issue for believers in Jesus who come from a Muslim background. "Anyone who has a conscience difficulty with this confession probably should leave Islam," Randy said. The believers Randy worked with were still discussing this issue.

I asked many more questions about their practices and beliefs. I was also very interested in how traditional Muslims perceive these new believers.

"A lot of stuff is tolerated within Muslim culture," Randy told me. "There are a lot of different Islamic beliefs. It's when you choose to leave the Muslim community that you really face problems."

I was having a hard time accepting that these people had proper biblical beliefs. I asked Randy, "What about heretical beliefs? How do these people stay true to what the Bible teaches?"

Randy talked about trusting the Holy Spirit in the process. He seemed convinced that the Holy Spirit and the Bible would guide the new believers eventually in the right directions. He protested that he, as a Westerner, was not the one to tell them what was "right" when it comes to their culture. "As a Westerner, I don't realize how deeply embedded I am in my own cultural sins. What if we as Westerners were required to leave all of these sins before we could become truly obedient? Where would that leave us?"

At one point, Randy leaned closer across the table and asked me a question. "At Pentecost, after Peter preached, how many of his listeners became Christians?"[3]

I thought back through my Bible reading and the many Sunday school classes I'd attended growing up as a preacher's kid. I came up with a guess. "Was it two thousand?"

With just the faintest smile, Randy said, "Zero. Most of them woke up that day and called themselves Jews. They all went to sleep that night calling themselves Jews." He explained that the term "Christian" wasn't coined until later.

It was a trick question, but a question with a point. According to Randy, the Bible doesn't teach that we have to call ourselves Christians.

The Word "Christian"

I went back to Colorado with my head spinning. I realized that one key part of Randy's story was the use of the word "Christian." Or rather, the startling abandonment of that label. If I could accept that alone, it seemed as though it would have far-reaching consequences. In a world where the word "Christian" has been filled with all kinds of nonbiblical meanings, could we simply invite people to follow Jesus but not use the word?

The implications were staggering. To understand why, it's important to face some depressing statistics. They are depressing, at least, for anyone interested in giving people an opportunity to investigate the person of Jesus and the teaching of the Bible. As a mission researcher, I was quite familiar with these numbers.

So far, surveys show that the people who have not yet heard and received the message about Jesus mostly fall into three groups: Muslims, Hindus, and Buddhists. Just using the guidebook *Operation World*, it is easy to see the stark reality of how little progress has been made. Although many Muslims, Buddhists, and high-caste Hindus have become Christians, the percentages are still small. In most of the countries where these religious groups dominate, the percentage of Christians has been stubbornly stuck at 4 percent or less.

The late mission strategist Ralph Winter put this situation bluntly. "To an awesome, serious degree," he wrote, "Christian mission has thus far dead-ended in these three major blocks: Hindus, Muslims, and Buddhists—and I don't think we are facing this fact very effectively."[4]

Dead-ended. That was a pretty sobering image to describe the progress of the gospel among the majority of the people who have yet to hear an explanation about Jesus, a group numbering over 2.5 billion.

The question I wondered about during the summer of 1998 was, could the word "Christian" have anything to do with these statistics?

That might sound like an irreverent question to ask. After all, the term "Christian" originally meant "those belonging to Christ," so to me it seemed like an appropriate and honorable term to use.[5] But I kept reading that the way I thought about "Christianity" from my upbringing in Canada and the United States was different from the way people in other nations viewed the word.

In the Muslim world, for example, it's not that the word "Christian" has become all bad for everyone, but it does produce a negative connotation for most. John Travis, a seminary professor who worked in an Asian Muslim country for more than twenty years, wrote, "While some Muslims may associate Christianity with the love and selfless living of Mother Teresa and relief organizations, most tend to focus on negative aspects of present-day Western culture like immodest dress, sexual promiscuity, disrespect of elders, indulgence in alcohol, Hollywood violence, narcotics and pornography."[6]

One of my coworkers from Asia said that most of his Muslim friends assume nearly all the pop stars from the West are Christians. He said he can ask almost any Muslim, "Is Lady Gaga a Christian?" and the person will usually say "Yes." When people make this assumption, they consider nearly all of the sensational behavior of stars and starlets that fills the tabloids as reflecting Christian values.

For many Muslim, Hindu, and Buddhist people, to become "Christian" means to leave behind their own cultural identity and to join that immoral Western way of life. It means joining a foreign culture just as much as it means becoming a believer in the teachings of the Bible.

For the people Randy worked with, not using the word "Christian" meant they could stay within their culture. It wasn't just about a word.

Randy told me he didn't feel compelled to use the word "Christian" because Jesus didn't command His followers to use any particular label. Jesus called His followers "disciples," "friends," "children of the kingdom," "children of light," and other names, but He didn't command that they use a label to distinguish themselves from other Jews. Although Paul used the term "follower of the Way" when speaking with Governor Felix, he didn't call for the use of one particular label in the assemblies of believers he worked with.[7]

So it seems the Bible gives room to use the word "Christian" or not to use it. As I read more and reflected more on what I had encountered with Randy, I decided that in this one matter at least—their using or not using the word "Christian"—they were incorporating a biblical approach. I also thought that if people from these community-oriented cultures have a negative view of what "Christian" culture means, and if they no longer have to take on the label "Christian" to become "one who belongs to Christ," that change alone could remove an enormous barrier.

Hope for the "Nones"

Then I started thinking about neighborhoods closer to home. Could the methods Randy and others were using on the other side of the world make a difference in the lives of people in my own country? I wondered what nonbiblical barriers young people face all around me, even in the houses across the street from mine, as they think about what Jesus and the Bible might mean for them.

It's an important question because those young men and women are leaving Christianity in record numbers. Young people are abandoning the church and they're not coming back. This isn't like the normal youthful exploration and then return. This is worse.

According to the 2012 Pew Research study "'Nones' on the Rise," more than one-third of Americans ages eighteen to twenty-two now call themselves religiously unaffiliated. When asked to name their religious affiliation, they say "none." Young people today are twice as likely to be religiously unaffiliated as young Baby Boomers were back in the '70s.[8]

This dramatic drift away from religious affiliation is happening despite the fact that a healthy majority (64 percent) of American youth say they are "absolutely certain" of God's existence.[9]

Perhaps one reason for this shift away from organized religion is that the "nones" see religion in a relatively negative light. According to the Pew study, "They are much more likely than the public overall to say that churches and other organizations are too concerned with money and power, too focused on rules, and too involved in politics."

For them, a word like "Christian" carries baggage. For them, as for Muslims and Hindus, such a word means much more than simply a description of faith. A 2007 Barna Research study found that the religiously unaffiliated held negative attitudes toward Christianity, the same kind of negative predispositions Randy has found in the Muslim community. In their report, they quoted one young "none" who said, "Most people I meet assume that 'Christian' means very conservative, entrenched in their thinking, antigay, anti-choice, angry, violent, illogical, empire builders; they want to convert everyone, and they generally cannot live peacefully with anyone who doesn't believe what they believe."[10]

I thought, if people are increasingly stepping away from organized Christianity, could it be that new ideas from places like Bangladesh and Thailand could provide an answer?

The people Randy and others are working with do things in their own cultural ways. Freed from the obligation to call themselves "Christians," they follow biblical faith in ways that are refreshingly different. They meet in unusual places, express themselves creatively, and use art and festivals innovatively. Might some of the unaffiliated "nones" in the United States come back to Jesus if they didn't have to enter traditional Christian culture to find Him? Could they benefit from alternatives to the word "Christian" to identify themselves? Could they also benefit from other insights from overseas? Could they find ways to follow Jesus that fit within their own styles and meeting places?

In the last decade, I've felt compelled to travel the world to try to answer these questions. What I've discovered has exceeded what I wondered about.

We are in the midst of a bursting out of creativity in faith in Christ. It's happening in places most of us haven't seen. What's happening holds the promise for new dimensions of faith in Christ as we see that faith lived out in diverse ways in other cultures. I believe that through these new insights our loved ones who are wandering can discover new ways to find Jesus, the transformation we long to see in the world can actually happen, and we can grow in ways we haven't been able to imagine before.

In order to see how, I invite you to join me on my journey of discovery. Together we'll travel to a city on the banks of the Ganges. We'll join a jamaat that meets in a kitchen in Bangladesh. We'll walk through a temple with a monk in Thailand. After our travels, we'll analyze four principles that can help us break down boundaries that keep us and the people we love from finding Jesus and the vitality He can give us. Then we'll dream together about what this new revival in faith could look like in our own lives.

But first, we'll look closer at the cultural box that surrounds faith in Jesus. We'll meet one of the people in the United States who has purposely chosen to leave the church behind. For that, we'll visit the Christian mecca of Colorado Springs.

2

A Taste of Something New

On a frosty Sunday morning in Colorado Springs, Craig Suderman and I held the door for Josh Kennard, the owner of Lofty's coffee shop, as he carried boxes from his car into the building. Josh was opening his café for the day.

Craig and I followed Josh into the shop and found a table. As Craig and I talked, Josh turned on the lights and music, started the coffee grinder, and adjusted the thermostat.

At this time of morning, people across this city, the hometown of dozens of Christian ministries, were waking up and making different preparations. They were getting dressed, getting the kids fed, and getting ready to go to church.

Craig, as usual, was not one of them. After thirty-five years of church attendance, mission training, and ministry leadership, Craig had walked away from all of it. He didn't attend any church anymore. I had come to Lofty's to find out why.

He had told me to look for the guy trying to grow a beard, and he did in fact have a short beard. He was wearing a brown-striped knit hat, an orange jacket, khaki pants, and hiking shoes. He ordered Devonshire Breakfast tea, I asked for tea as well, and we clutched our hot mugs as we got acquainted.

Now forty years old, Craig told me he had grown up in a small farming town in Kansas surrounded by Mennonite culture. As a boy, he learned about God. What he remembered most, though, were stories of the martyrs. He went to a Mennonite college nearby, but he didn't attend a church.

In his midtwenties, Craig finally heard the message about Jesus in a way that connected with him. He had moved to another state, was in the midst of graduate studies, and had broken up with his girlfriend. In a sermon at a Baptist church, he heard about Jesus as though he were hearing the story for the first time. He had an awakening.

Soon he also had a thriving career as a nurse anesthetist. He worked in rural North Dakota not far from the Canadian border. But before long he began wondering if something was missing. He had already achieved most of his goals. He started thinking, "I say Jesus is Lord, but I really spend more time on myself than on Him."

After his sister told him about a mission training program, Craig found a subcontractor to take over his practice, and he traveled to Colorado Springs to study mission strategy for five months. During that time, he got involved in a large church in the city. People were flocking to the church. It had a global vision and gave those who attended the sense of being at the hub of a movement. Craig wanted to become part of that. He wanted to make decisions based not so much on his economic well-being as on his social and spiritual environment. After the mission training ended, he decided to move his nurse anesthetist practice to Colorado Springs.

That's when Craig's enthusiasm for institutional Christianity began to decline. He looked around at all the ministries in the church and tried to find the one that was the most culturally relevant, that was loving people in a significant way. He picked the youth ministry. "From the outside," Craig recalled, "it seemed like, wow, they are really making a difference in these kids' lives."

Craig began by recruiting leaders for junior high ministry. After three years, he started to see a trend. "Every year we were not getting the results we wanted, and every year we were tweaking the system." There were only a handful of adult volunteers, even though the church numbered many thousands. Mostly Craig saw high school kids mentoring the junior high boys and girls.

He asked himself, "What kind of Christians is this system really producing?" Without the adult leaders, the church staff couldn't do in-depth discipleship and instead had to rely on large-group events. "Mass ministry," Craig observed, "is a lot of pulling populist levers. It's that collective spirituality that people can find an identity in, but at the end of the day, it kind of leaves them disillusioned."

The junior high pastor understood this predicament and gave Craig permission to invest deeply in a small group of boys. Craig could do with a few what they would like to do with all the kids if only they had enough volunteers. By the time Craig's boys reached high school, Craig looked forward to moving up with them to the church's flagship youth program. The high school leaders were putting on conferences for youth groups from other churches, they were going on mission trips, and this was supposed to be a model youth ministry. But instead, Craig found the same lack of adult volunteers. And he didn't find the same openness to his model of deep one-on-one relationships with the boys he had been discipling. "I got a taste of being marginalized and isolated and being shut down," Craig recalled.

Eventually Craig came to regard the big youth program as a show. In Craig's view, they would celebrate the stories of kids who probably would have come to faith even without the church's ministry, and they would overlook the other kids who had drifted away. "They say this generation is the most marketed generation in the world," Craig told me. "Everybody is trying to sell them something. We're just another voice in the crowd." Craig said the kids he met were hypersensitive to hypocrisy and manipulation. He began to develop the same distaste for these qualities in the church activities he participated in, like small groups, mission training programs, and weekly youth gatherings. "It's one of the things that made me leave youth ministry."

When Craig left the high school program, he realized he was also leaving the church. He had stopped going to the main service on Sunday mornings. "I wasn't really into what was going on there," Craig said. "I think following Jesus is more beautiful and true and meaningful and real than the experience of going to these gatherings on Sunday mornings."

The problem with church activities, Craig said, is that they don't connect with what he reads when he studies the Bible. "We say we're following Jesus, but if we really look at what Jesus did specifically, it looks nothing like that."

This frustrates Craig. "I'm so ill-prepared to do what I know the gospel shows me to do, and I have nowhere to look to lead the way."

He has been inspired by people called the "new monastics," who form communities to love their neighborhoods and work on issues like racial reconciliation or social justice. He left the church partly to give him the impetus to find such a community.

Craig wonders if, like the Pharisees, believers have come to a point where we need to recognize that God is bigger than our religion. "I think we try to love people with systems and institutions. And I really think loving this culture needs to be done outside of the institutional umbrella. That's why I think the church is just not up to the task."

Leaving the Church Behind

Craig is not alone in this conclusion. In fact, researchers have identified a growing number of people in the West who have chosen to leave the church behind. Like Craig, most of them (74 percent) grew up within a religious tradition, and many of them also retain core beliefs about God and the Bible. Two-thirds of them say they believe in God.[1]

The Gallup organization has been tracking the number of "unchurched" for more than eighty years, and they've discovered a persistent trend. To determine if a person is unchurched, the Gallup people ask two questions: "Do you happen to be a member of a church, synagogue, or mosque?" and "Apart from weddings, funerals, or special holidays . . . have you attended the church, synagogue, or mosque of your choice in the past six months?" If the respondent answers "no" to either of these questions, Gallup calls them "unchurched." Gallup's surveys show the number of unchurched steadily rising in the United States from 41 percent in 1978 to 46 percent in 2011.[2] In Canada and Britain, the percentage of unchurched is much higher: 66 percent of Canadians are unchurched and 80 percent of the British.[3]

The numbers become more disturbing when they are broken down by age, and when researchers ask not only if a person attends church but also if he or she will list any religious preference at all. In the last chapter, I mentioned a 2012 Pew Research Center study called "'Nones' on the Rise." This study made headlines by reporting, "One-fifth of the American public—and a third of adults under 30—are religiously unaffiliated, the highest percentages ever in Pew Research Center polling."[4] It's remarkable to think that one in three young adults in the United States will not list any religious preference.

Another recent Pew report found that of all religious categories, such as Catholics, Protestants, Muslims, and Mormons, the "religiously unaffiliated" category is growing the fastest in the United States.[5]

In their own studies, Gallup found almost the same statistics. They commented, "The rise in the religious 'nones' over time is one of the most significant trends in religious measurement in the United States."[6]

As a result of these trends, Christian families increasingly wonder what to do. If one in three young people now calls himself or herself religiously unaffiliated, and if most of these youth have grown up in the church, that means virtually every churchgoing family now feels this pain. In ever-increasing numbers, sons and daughters, brothers and sisters, cousins and nephews are choosing not to follow the Christian practices of their families.

Many who leave the church seem uninterested in coming back. A 2014 Barna Group study showed that less than half of Americans now see church attendance as even slightly important, and the young-adult Millennial generation shows the least appetite for church. Only two in ten Millennials mark church attendance as having any importance for them. A higher number of Millennials, 35 percent, express antichurch attitudes.[7]

More of the Same

It's clear that young people in the West are leaving the Christian church in record numbers. What's not clear is what to do about that. Most of the books and articles I've read about the growing number of unchurched in the West offer no real solution. Most of the authors provide analysis but not much hope.

In the foreword of a recent book, George Barna, the founder of Barna Research, commented on the shortage of answers to this problem of young people leaving Christianity behind. He stated that Christian innovations mostly involve repackaging. Referring to young people leaving the church, Barna asked, "Those involved know what they are shifting from—lifeless, institutional forms of faith. . . . But what are they shifting to?"[8]

Barna suggested, have Christians just been trying to give youth more of the same? If they like loud music, let's make the music louder. If kids want to have fun, let's have lots of fun. Barna said these seem like "marketing strategies to perform the same activities in different ways."[9]

I've wondered, maybe we keep giving more of the same because "the same" is all we know.

The sad thing is that, until recently, you wouldn't discover many new ideas even by traveling to other countries. The Christian landscape across the United States and Europe looks pretty much the same wherever you go. And in Asia and Africa, Christianity looks remarkably similar. In some cases you see the 1950s American church all over again.

I've discovered this on many of my travels. In 2005, I sat in the back of a Presbyterian church in Taiwan. Just as the service was about to begin, a procession of men wearing suits entered from the back. They walked up the center aisle, filed into the front row, paused for a moment, and sat down in unison. Even before my friend translated for me what was happening, I knew what was going on.

It was communion Sunday. These men were elders. They were there to serve the communion. I knew because I once was one of those men. I did exactly the same thing when I served as a Presbyterian elder in California. I wore one of those suits. I took my place in the procession from the back. I entered the front row, waited, and sat down with the others.

The rest of that service in Taiwan followed precisely the liturgy I knew so well from California. They sang the same songs, using Mandarin words. They took the offering in the same way. They even played the same kind of music while the communion elements were passed.

Afterward, as the parishioners mingled outside the high-rise building that housed the church, I looked across the street and saw a Buddhist temple. The bright reds and greens and ornate carvings of its architecture stood in stark contrast to the beige pews in the sanctuary I had just left.

I've experienced that same kind of culture clash all over the world. Almost everywhere, Christianity looks the same. People walk into a building, they sit in rows, they sing songs, a preacher speaks, and they go home. They usually keep their shoes on, in spite of the fact that in many cultures people show respect for spiritual places by slipping off their flip-flops at the door or untying their shoes and placing them in neat racks. I've seen the same Christian pattern in churches in Thailand, Mexico, Brazil, Zambia, South Korea, and many other countries. Somehow, Christianity has exported itself in the form of little bits of Europe or America, and these bits live on as foreign enclaves in Africa, Asia, and the Middle East.

Way back in 1912, Roland Allen, a missionary to China, looked around the world and saw these European-American customs in country after country. Exasperated, he wrote, "Everywhere we see the same types. . . . There has been no new revelation. There has been no new discovery of new aspects of the gospel, no new unfolding of new forms of Christian life."[10]

How did this happen?

According to professor and author Charles Kraft, mission in the "modern missionary era," which he dates from roughly 1790 on, involved an encounter between the "Christian" culture of Europe and America and the "pagan" cultures of the rest of the world. "The cultures of non-Western peoples (and especially their religions) were seen as evil and needing to be stamped out if the gospel was to be effective."[11] For example, New England Puritans in their work with Native Americans sought to bring about "civilization and Christianity." This slogan meant that the proper way to obey biblical faith was "to be made over in the likeness of European culture."

In many countries, that European likeness remained even after the foreigners left. According to Professor Kraft, when the missionaries tried to pass on their work to native peoples, the Indian or African or Chinese Christian leaders simply maintained the European customs.[12]

As a result, today the format for faith in Jesus appears pretty much the same all over the world. It looks that way because, with the best of intentions, it was exported that way.

The non-Christian populations of most of those countries still view Christianity as a foreign intruder. One mission professor remarked that "the vast majority of Indians remain indifferent to or antagonistic to Western expressions of Christianity. Even in some of its most vibrant forms, the Christianity planted in India is viewed as cultural and religious opposition and an outpost of Western civilization and religion."[13]

A Taste of Something New

Is this the way God intended faith in Christ to appear? In the picture of all the nations around the throne in Revelation 7:9, people come there from every tribe, nation, ethnic group, and language. They must be distinguishable from each other. They haven't become completely homogeneous. Gathering around the throne, they all recognize that the sacrifice of Jesus is the reason they are there. But I have to believe God enjoys their diversity. I believe it because of the world God made and because of what I learn about God in the pages of His book. The God who made every snowflake different, and who paid such attention to the festivals and customs of His holy nation, and who expressed His love for all nations and all ethnic groups over and over throughout the Bible—surely this God loves the variety of the peoples He made.[14]

Yet for some reason, the followers of Jesus have stifled cultural diversity in Christianity for centuries.

I think this is one reason that, according to the surveys, growing numbers of young people have become bored with the Christian faith. In a 2007 study by Barna Research, two-thirds of unchurched youth called Christianity boring, and even one-quarter of young Christians used that same word to describe the Christianity that surrounds them.[15]

Could there exist inside the growing number of unchurched nones, and perhaps inside many routine churchgoers as well, a cry for something new, but they don't know what that new thing is?

I wonder if there's a parallel with the appetite in the West for ethnic cuisine. Could it be that Christianity, as it grew up in Europe and America, developed its own kind of flavor? It has become like good old European meat, potatoes, and gravy. Or to Americanize it, like the hamburger. Christianity exported that flavor wherever it went. So now, no matter where you go, Christianity basically smells like and tastes like hamburgers and french fries. It might have been altered a little bit, just as McDonald's adds salsas or sauces or vegetables depending on the country they're in, but it's still basically burgers and fries wherever you go. Just as the Golden Arches connote a foreign food, now Christian steeples give off that same aroma.

That's bad if people think that to follow Jesus they have to give up their falafel or their tempura and eat nothing but the Big Mac. But it's also bad for the land of hamburgers if that's all there is to eat. That's the other side of this.

As I've watched the growth of the approach Randy told me about, I've observed that it has created much more than a different label. I have seen new forms of Christian life emerging. When people have tried to obey the Bible within their own culture, without having to join the "Christian" culture, they have begun to follow Christ in new ways.

Faith is breaking out of its colonial box. This is not happening for the first time, of course. People like N. V. Tilak in India and Don Richardson in Irian Jaya pioneered similar approaches decades ago. But now the breakout is gathering momentum and going in directions no one has seen before. It is emerging in newfound variety and creativity. And most people don't know about it. Other than a handful of field-workers and mission professionals, very few people are aware of what is going on.

Could it be that these new believers, as they follow Jesus in new ways, will discover aspects of the Bible no one in the West has seen before? Could it be they will bring new ways of gathering or new ways of expressing themselves that people in other parts of the world might find inspiring? Could they offer new ideas to people like Craig in Colorado Springs?

It will probably seem strange and unlikely at first. It's as unlikely as a boy who hid cooked spinach under his napkin at home growing up to choose a big green dollop of *saag paneer* at an Indian buffet. Many of the ideas in this book will seem odd and uncomfortable, but that's often the way change begins.

To give you a framework to evaluate the unusual approaches you will experience in the next chapters, I'd like to introduce a helpful tool. It's called the C-Scale. It was developed by John Travis and

The C-Scale

C1	**Traditional Church Using Outsider Language.** Believers may dress in Western clothes, sit on chairs or pews, listen to a sermon in a language that is not their mother tongue, and might sing hymns or contemporary Christian worship songs.
C2	**Traditional Church Using Insider Language.** Believers use Western dress, music, and building style, but the service takes place in the language of the local population. According to John Travis, "The majority of churches located in the Muslim world today are C1 or C2."
C3	**Christ-Centered Communities Using Insider Language and Religiously Neutral Cultural Forms.** Believers dress in local clothing and might incorporate folk music and artwork into their meetings, but they would not incorporate aspects of the culture that are associated with Islam. These believers call themselves "Christians."
C4	**Christ-Centered Communities Using Insider Language and Biblically Permissible Cultural and Religious Forms.** In addition to local clothing and art forms, these churches would also incorporate religious customs. In the Islamic world, these customs could include praying with raised hands, keeping the Ramadan fast, avoiding pork, wearing Islamic dress, etc. In many of these fellowships, believers use a unique term to describe themselves, like "followers of Isa the Messiah."
C5	**Christ-Centered Communities of Muslims Who Have Accepted Jesus as Lord and Savior Yet Remain a Part of the Muslim Community.** These believers use all the customs found in C4 fellowships yet remain culturally, socially, and legally Muslim. The community views them as Muslims. "Aspects of Islamic theology which are incompatible with the Bible are rejected or reinterpreted," noted John Travis.
C6	**Small Christ-Centered Communities of Secret/Underground Believers.** In Islamic settings, these believers call themselves Muslims and are seen as Muslims by the community. There is little or no opportunity for open fellowship.

Adapted from John Travis, "The C1 to C6 Spectrum," *Evangelical Missions Quarterly* (October 1998), 407–8.

published in 1998, not long after my talk with Randy in Thailand. Travis looked at all the different types of "Christ-centered communities" (hence the "C" in the scale) he saw in the Muslim country where he lived and created a continuum to describe them. Travis divided the spectrum into six parts.

At one end, C1 and C2 describe the most common types of Christian churches in the Muslim world. These churches predominantly use Western culture such as hymns and European-style clothing. Then, from C3 to C5, the fellowships Travis studied increasingly incorporated the local culture. At C3 the practices these believers used were nonreligious, such as folk music. At C4 the fellowships incorporated Islamic customs into their practices. Some of them kept the Ramadan fast. At C4 many of them also did not call themselves Christians but used a unique term like "followers of Isa the Messiah." At C5 they called themselves Muslims and were seen as Muslims by the community. They would change some of their Islamic beliefs, however. At C6, at the extreme end of the scale, Travis described secret believers, those who lived a public life as Muslims but believed in Jesus in private. They usually did not meet with other followers of Jesus.

While Travis's intent with this spectrum was to describe and encourage a wide range of diverse approaches within the Muslim world, the real story that emerged from his article is found in C5. This description, which appeared in a respected journal, made known an approach and a type of fellowship that had gone largely unnoticed until this point. All of the other types of Christ-centered communities were fairly well known.

Also, by putting C5 on a spectrum, Travis gave these fellowships equal footing with traditional C1 and C2 churches. He implied that this approach and type of fellowship had legitimacy equal to the more commonly accepted types. This was a paradigm-shaking assertion that created many kinds of reactions, both for and against.

It was one thing not to use the word "Christian," but for believers in Jesus to still call themselves Muslims? Wasn't that deceptive?

Theologian John Stott asked the question: "Is it possible to conceive of converts becoming followers of Jesus without so forsaking their Islamic culture that they are regarded as traitors? Can we even contemplate Jesus mosques instead of churches and Jesus Muslims instead of Christians?"[16]

I still have many of my own questions about these approaches to expressing faith in Christ. In the next four chapters, I'll introduce you to believers I met in every major religious group, all across the C-Scale, including those who worship in C5 communities. As I go, I'll address some of the questions I faced.

With this road map, I invite you to come and see for yourself what I have had the privilege to see. On my travels I was given access to places most visitors would not be allowed to go.

Smell the aromas. Use your imagination. Consider if what you're seeing and hearing could enrich faith in Jesus.

To start with, I invite you to come to India, and to join me at something called a *satsang*.

Part One

THE INSIDERS

3

The Satsang

In Arun and Vishal's apartment, two living room chairs had been pushed into corners. Carpets and mats covered the blue linoleum floor.

I entered the room and Arun, a young Indian man in his mid-twenties, greeted me. He had a short beard and was wearing an Indian-style shirt with a beaded necklace and black trousers. He welcomed me to the *satsang*. I took off my shoes, left them by the door, and found a place to sit on a mat.

I had been told the word "satsang" combines two Sanskrit words, *sat* meaning "truth" and *sanga* meaning "community." In the Hindu world, the satsang remains a common religious gathering, a fellowship of seekers after truth.

Arun greeted the other people who were now arriving. Most of the other eight guests were Indian and many were wearing jeans and short-sleeved, collared shirts. Since this was a gathering for male college students, almost all the men who arrived were in their twenties like Arun and his roommate, Vishal. They all kicked off their sandals and joined me on the floor in the living room.

Even though the sun had gone down, fans did little to cool the guests in the ninety-degree heat. At this time of year in India, at the beginning of the hot season, the evenings didn't seem much cooler than midday.

We formed a rough circle around a metal plate in the center of the room. On the plate, two incense sticks burned in their silver holder, and a few marigolds formed an orange and yellow circle. Next to the plate, a small wooden stand held an open book. Arun sat cross-legged before the stand.

He smiled at everyone and, in Hindi, welcomed them cheerfully. He asked if anyone had suggestions of songs they'd like to include.

The group began singing, first without any accompaniment. Then a man named Pradip, who had picked up a small drum called a *dholak*, began to play. Vishal also joined in, playing two small silver cymbals called *manjira*. The others clapped and sang with increasing enthusiasm as the song picked up speed. This style of song, called a *bhajan*, often involves call and repeat and is used in Hindu worship.

In Hindi, we sang these words:

> *Deep jale, Prabhu naam rahe,*
> *Mere mandir mein, mandir mein*
> *Saanj sabere yeh man gaaye*
> *Yesu teraa naam, Prabhu Yesu teraa naam.*

In English, the words mean:

> Keep the lamp burning so the Lord's name will remain,
> Remain in the temple, remain in my heart.
> In the morning and in the evening my soul sings to you,
> Yeshu, your name, Lord Yeshu, your name.[1]

We sang four more songs. Sometimes Arun commented on the previous song. Other times, members of the group led with one of their favorites. A boy in his late teens sitting next to Arun sang with great feeling and started one of the songs just as another ended.

Arun then talked for about twenty minutes. He began with a story about two men who walked into a mango grove. One measured a piece of fruit and then left. The other picked a mango and tasted it. Arun asked, "Who really knows about the mango?"

"The second man," answered one of the men in the group.

"Yes. It was the one who ate it and didn't just study it," Arun said. Then he added, "We can study about God and never really know God. We need to experience Him and come to know Him." Arun then told the story of Peter getting out of the boat and walking on the water. Arun said that by going to Jesus, Peter experienced the power of God.

With that, Arun asked if anyone had prayer requests. Several prayed, including some who had seemed less familiar with the songs.

They closed with a short chant, and then Vishal brought out chai, sweet milky tea, in little cups. He also passed around two metal plates, one with cookies and one with fried-lentil snacks.

As the group visited with each other, I didn't realize that in the days before this satsang, Arun and Vishal had faced a difficult decision about one of the people in that room. Charan, the boy in his late teens who sang so eagerly, had come to this city to attend a school here. Like most of the others in the room, he heard about this group from friends at school. He enjoyed singing the bhajans. Charan had just been accepted into engineering college in a faraway city. He had heard about *jal sanskar*, which means "water sacrament," and had learned how *Sadguru Yeshu*, the Supreme Master Jesus, had commanded this ritual. He heard that jal sanskar was the guru's *diksha*, a teacher's initiation ceremony. Charan told Arun he wanted to commit himself to Sadguru Yeshu as his only guru, his only master. He declared, "Yes, yes, yes! I really am willing to do this." Charan said he very much wanted to go through jal sanskar before he left for the other school.

Arun told Jay, the leader of a small outreach team in this city, about Charan's desire.

Jay asked, "Do you really think he is a follower of Sadguru Yeshu, or is he all mixed up?" Jay had heard that one time when Charan went home to visit his family, he got in trouble for drawing crosses on the wall. At that time, Charan was struggling to figure out Christ and the cross. His Hindu parents became nervous that Charan might want to become a Christian. Charan comes from a prominent family in a neighboring state. They have a lot of land and servants.

"I think he really is a follower of Yeshu," Arun assured Jay. "He became a *bhakta*." In the Hindu community, a bhakta is a person who has become a devotee of a god, and sometimes of only one god. Arun explained, "He's so excited. He brings Bible stories he wants to share with me. 'I read this story about Sadguru Yeshu!' he says. He's memorizing Scriptures. He quotes them in prayer." Arun also told Jay how Charan had told him about the sin in his life, had wept about it, and had asked Yeshu for forgiveness. Arun and Charan had prayed a long time as Charan committed his life to Jesus.

Jay still pursed his lips with concern. Was Charan ready for Arun to give him jal sanskar? And was Arun the best person to do it? Arun is from a Christian background. What if Charan's family pressures Charan about this sacrament and finds out a Christian gave it to him? If Charan goes through jal sanskar, should Pradip go with him instead? Pradip comes from a Hindu Brahmin background and has become a Yeshu Bhakta. He's one of the elders in this community. Perhaps Pradip should be the one to go with Charan into the water. Jay had to decide quickly because Charan would leave soon.

Staying Hindu

It was because of Jay's invitation that I had come to this part of India. I had met Jay seven years before in Bali, Indonesia. At that time, he wore his reddish-brown hair in long dreadlocks, and had let his beard grow long and full. He looked to be about thirty. He wore an Indian-style shirt, a skirt-like wrap called a *lungi*, and flip-flops. He was carrying a simple shoulder bag made out of Indian cloth.

I thought, with some gray ash on his forehead, this guy could be a Hindu holy man. Without it, he could be a hippy surfer.

Jay told me he grew up in Coon Rapids, Minnesota. After he got some mission training in Texas, he came to India at the age of twenty-five bursting with ideas. He said he still remembered leaving the Delhi airport and walking out of the air-conditioning into the furnace blast outside. He looked at all the people watching travelers arrive, their faces pressed up against the chain-link fence. A week later, after driving past roadside shrines and imposing temples, and seeing places of worship for stones and trees, he said, "I was in shock. I was ready to flee this demonic land."

On Sunday, though, he breathed a sigh of relief when his hosts took him to church. He sat on the wooden pew and watched the Indian pastor, who was wearing a shirt and tie, lead the congregation through the familiar order of service. There were greetings, announcements, hymns, Bible readings, preaching, and an offering. Even though he couldn't understand the words, Jay felt comforted. "I was so pleased that the Good News had taken root in India, and people could come to this church and be saved."

I could understand Jay's reaction. I remembered the first time I visited a predominantly Hindu nation. I had camped with some Christians near a Hindu shrine, which contained an image of the goddess Kali. She had been painted deep blue and her red tongue was sticking out. In one of her four arms she held a severed head and in another a bloody knife. I couldn't imagine why anyone would worship such a figure. As I lay there in the dark and heard the chimes from the shrine blowing in the wind, it seemed I could feel the presence of evil.

At that time, I would have been surprised to hear what author H. L. Richard later told me: "Among many streams of belief among

Hindus, 'fluid monotheism' is a good description for the majority viewpoint."[2]

Monotheism? Don't Hindus worship millions of gods? According to books on world religions, although some Hindus do hold to pantheistic ideas, many Hindus have a concept of the Supreme God, called *Parameshwara*, or the ultimate reality, called Brahman or *Bhagwan*. Some Hindus would consider Vishnu or Shiva as the Ultimate, the Highest Lord.

Often a family will choose a specific god as the focus of their devotion. Although theoretically there are three ways to be saved from the cycle of reincarnation, H. L. Richard points to a scholarly consensus that in practice most Hindus use this way of devotion. This way is called bhakti.

In the midst of this ancient and pervasive Hindu culture, Indian Christians claim that the message about Jesus arrived two thousand years ago with the apostle Thomas. In the next few centuries, a Christian community grew up in South India. During the missionary era, under Roman Catholic and Protestant ministries, many of the lowest caste and tribal communities responded to the gospel in the greatest numbers. Today approximately 80 percent of Indian Christians come from this background.[3]

With most outreach in India focusing on tribal areas and the lower castes, the upper castes have remained largely untouched. For example, of the fifty million Brahmins, who represent the highest priestly class, there are only eighteen thousand known believers in Christ.[4] That's only 0.036 percent who have become Christians.

Part of the problem is that much of Indian Christianity still looks like that church Jay visited in Delhi. It looks like a foreign import.

According to author Dayanand Bharati, Indian Christianity has almost no Indianness in it. Bharati, who became a devoted Jesus-follower after being raised Hindu, wrote that generations of Indian Christians grow up in the church and don't even see its foreignness anymore. "In India," Bharati wrote, "one can hardly find an Indian church because here we have Greek philosophy,

Roman administration, . . . German theology, European culture and *nothing Indian*."[5]

In his book, *Living Water and Indian Bowl*, Bharati objects to wearing shoes in church, standing rather than sitting to speak about God, Western music rather than bhajans, shirts and ties rather than traditional Indian clothing, the avoidance of useful words from the Hindu vocabulary, and many more cultural offenses.

Through the years, several pioneers have tried to break out of this Western mold, such as Roberto di Nobili, Narayan Vaman Tilak, Brahmabandhab Upadhyay, and Sadhu Sundar Singh. Some of them have even explored whether a believer in Jesus can remain a Hindu.

Jay explained that a person can be a monotheist or an atheist and still fit under the Hindu umbrella. That's the reason Jay and a growing number of others believe a person can follow biblical faith and still call himself or herself a Hindu.

At a conference I attended, H. L. Richard argued that point strongly. "You can change your theology and still be Hindu," he asserted. He explained that the Hindu scriptures even provide room for different views about reincarnation, the one doctrine that most Hindus do agree on.[6]

"It's not about ideas. It's not about practices," Richard declared. "It's mostly about identity." Richard has become one of the most eloquent and forceful proponents of the approach in which Hindus follow Jesus within their Hindu communities.

It's not a hypothetical idea. According to *Operation World*, there may be millions of this kind of Hindu believer.[7]

In the early 1980s, a provocative study investigated Hindus who follow Jesus. After sixteen years of work in India, Lutheran pastor Herbert Hoefer became fascinated by the number of believers in Jesus who never came to a Christian church. He met some of them within their Hindu communities and discovered that they held fairly orthodox views of who Jesus is. Hoefer wanted to know what these people believed and how many of them there were, so he commissioned a statistical study of the southern India city of Chennai. His findings, which he published in his book *Churchless Christianity*, were surprising. Hoefer discovered that the number of Hindus who said they worshiped "only Jesus" was almost exactly the same as the number of Christians in the city. Given the city's population at the time, Hoefer estimated the number of Hindu believers in Jesus at 156,000.[8]

That was just in one city, a city located in the region of India where this phenomenon is probably most prevalent.

Some Hindus who follow Jesus in this way have started meeting together. They call themselves names like Yeshu Bhaktas, or Khrist Bhakts, indicating their bhakti devotion to one God. Teams that Jay has worked with in a city in North India have started forty satsang fellowship groups with a total of about five hundred believers. Jay told me of a Yeshu ashram where fifteen hundred villagers meet every Sunday for a satsang and more than four thousand come to their monthly meeting.

As I walked along the banks of the Ganges and through the narrow alleys of the city I was visiting, I tried to understand what it could be like to follow Jesus within Hinduism.

Early one morning, I walked down to the water to see the city from the river's point of view. In the pink, early morning light, men and women of all ages waded into the water. They cupped the water and drew it up over their bodies. They pursed their hands before them in prayer and slowly sank straight down under the surface. They came up dripping and murmuring chants or prayers.

I wanted to know, if people follow Jesus, or Sadguru Yeshu, within Hinduism, what do they actually believe? And what is their life like?

Pradip's Accident

I didn't have to go far to find a person to talk to. Pradip, the drum player from the satsang I attended, agreed to tell me his story. He comes from a Brahmin background and still considers himself a Hindu. His account about how he met Jesus turned out to be more dramatic than I expected.

He met with me on the roof of a five-story building. We sat on patio furniture on the flat cement roof, and looked out over potted plants at rows of neighboring dwellings and the Ganges in the distance.

Pradip, a thirtyish, burly man, told about one frightful night during his senior year of postgraduate studies in psychology. On December 23 at 11:30 in the evening, Pradip was heading home on his motorcycle. He had just finished a day of arranging housing for people who were arriving for a psychology conference. As he crossed a railroad track, a car crashed into him going about forty miles per hour. The impact hurtled Pradip twenty-five feet down the road. He lay there dimly aware that he was bleeding profusely from a head wound.

Three drivers of auto rickshaws, the three-wheeled taxis, helped him get to the hospital. As he lay on the gurney in the emergency room, the medical staff tried frantically to stop the bleeding. The last words he heard before he passed out were, "I don't think we can save him. He's going to die."

Up until this point, Pradip had been a bit unclear about what would happen to him after death. He had grown up a strict Hindu. His grandfather had been famous throughout the city for his Hindu devotion. Pradip himself carried on this faith with enthusiasm. Each day he would dip a container of Ganges water and take it to the Shiva temple. He would sing bhajans to Shiva and worship him for one or two hours every day. In addition, he would worship Ram for another hour.

When he went to university, Pradip wanted to grow spiritually. He also wanted to learn to play an instrument. One of his friends attended a Yeshu satsang and invited him to come along. Pradip agreed to go. He wanted to learn to play the manjira and he wanted to learn more English.

He came to the satsang with this mind-set: "Yes, Sadguru Yeshu is also one god." He believed in Parameshwara, the all-powerful God. He revered Parameshwara as the *paramaatmaa*, or Supreme Spirit, the creator of the earth, the sun, and the moon. He believed that Parameshwara could decide to be born wherever he wants to. In India he could be Ram, Krishna, or Shiva. In Israel he could come as Yeshu.

This view didn't change when Pradip started attending the satsang. What changed were his feelings toward Yeshu. The leader of the satsang asked Pradip to read from the Hindi Bible. Pradip read out loud, and he also heard stories told during the satsang. But what really moved him was the singing. Somehow when he sang, the statements he'd heard began to enter his heart. For example, he was struck by the fact that "no other god came here for giving sacrifice." Others came as kings, but Yeshu lived a simple life. Pradip didn't like how some Brahmin people don't want to touch the lower castes. Jesus was different. He touched an unclean woman and even a leper.

When Pradip sang the bhajans, these facts came alive for him. One time in particular, Chris Hale, the founder of the musical group Aradhna, came to visit. Hale, who grew up in Nepal, plays the sitar. The music of Aradhna features bhajans played in an East/West fusion. At the satsang Pradip played the manjira as Hale led the singing.

"That time I closed my eyes, and I can't explain it. This feeling came in my heart," Pradip recalled.

As he tried to explain to me what he felt, he used two Hindi words, *daya* and *karuna*. He said, if a person passed a beggar who had no clothes to wear during the cold season, a person with daya might give clothes sympathetically, but a person with karuna would give the clothes and would feel the beggar's pain. "It is karuna if you are able to go inside his personality," Pradip said.

When he sang the bhajan, Pradip realized "Sadguru Yeshu was able to do that." He was overwhelmed with the karuna of Yeshu.

Pradip almost couldn't contain this feeling. "I thought, oh, now I will start crying. But I'm not crying, only I'm feeling. If I had to put a word to this feeling it would be love."

Through these emotions of song, Pradip found that Yeshu now occupied in his heart a place as high as the other gods he had worshiped since childhood.

Then one night the car smashed into him and the world went black.

Pradip felt himself moving from a light area toward a dark part of a room. He sensed that the light was life and the dark was death. As he felt himself slowly falling into the darkness, suddenly somebody took hold of his hand. He felt a soft grip that jerked him back toward the light. He couldn't see the person's face, but could see that he wore a white kurta, a long Indian shirt.

Pradip became aware that he was lying in a hospital room. He was alive!

During the two months of bed rest that followed, Pradip became convinced that the person who pulled him back to life was Sadguru Yeshu. Shiva, he thought, lives naked. Ram has a bow and arrow. Vishnu sits on a big snake. Hanuman has a tail like a monkey's. Only Sadguru Yeshu has that white robe.

Pradip also had time to ponder the reasons to believe. Unlike the stories of the Hindu gods, Pradip realized that the stories of Sadguru Yeshu could be proven. He thought about the Old Testament prophecies and how Sadguru Yeshu fulfilled them. He thought about the baptism of Sadguru Yeshu and how the voice of Parameshwara said, "This is my Son whom I love." He thought about how practical people like Americans and the British would want proof before believing. And many of them believe.

"In India," he said, grabbing a leaf of a plant next to him, "I could say this is god. I got something yesterday from this plant, so this is a god. Now others will come here to also worship this plant." People from other countries, he thought, want more proof.

Pradip determined that he would bind himself to Yeshu alone. He would stop going to any other temple. He concluded that "The real Parameshwara is the Sadguru Yeshu only. There is only one Holy Spirit and the rest are from the devil."

I asked Pradip if he thought he had become a Christian like the Americans and the British.

He said, "I never told anybody I am a Christian. I said I am a Sadguru Yeshu Bhakta. I'm a Hindu. Now I'm Pradip. Before I was Pradip. I can drink water in the glass. I can drink water in the bowl. I'm a Hindu. But I'm a devotee of Sadguru Yeshu."

One of the first things Pradip did was to start a satsang in his own home. His parents agreed because they also recognized the hand of Yeshu in saving their son. During Pradip's coma, which had lasted for several weeks, they had exhausted their finances on Hindu-style cures and the best of traditional medical care. Only when Arun came and asked if he could pray in the name of Sadguru Yeshu did Pradip come back to life.

Pradip's mother told him, "You went to the satsang on Sunday, so, yes, Sadguru Yeshu also liked you and He didn't want you to die now."

Pradip said when his mother and father participate in the satsang, they also enjoy the bhajans, the songs, the most.

Now Pradip thinks deeply about how to communicate the message of Yeshu to his friends and his family in a way they can understand. Recently he used a cup analogy and a word analogy to try to explain the Trinity to a friend. The friend asked Pradip why he couldn't just worship Parameshwara directly, why he needed Sadguru Yeshu.

"We should think more and more every day, how can I tell, by which way can I explain this for every person," Pradip told me earnestly.

With real feeling, he expressed confidence that the slow progress he sees in his family will lead them to the same conclusions he's come to. "I think sure that day will come when my parents will say, yes, the real Parameshwara is Sadguru Yeshu."

The Jal Sanskar

The morning after the satsang I attended, Pradip, Arun, and Charan arose very early. At 5:00 a.m. they arrived at the Ganges. Already many people were in the water, preparing to do their morning *puja*, or worship, with the rising of the sun. The three men, bare chested, wearing the *lungi* wraps, waded into the water until it reached their waists. With their backs to the city, they gazed out over the river. Pradip stood next to Charan. They prayed together. Then Charan, without Pradip touching him, went straight down under the water and back up again.

Pradip came close to Charan and whispered in his ear the guru mantra. This part of a Hindu guru *diksha*, or initiation ceremony, usually involves a special mantra for the initiate to learn, though the person may not understand what the words mean. In the jal sanskar, or water sacrament ceremony, the Hindu believers in Jesus have turned this mantra into the giving of a special Bible verse. During the night before the jal sanskar, Pradip had been praying, asking Sadguru Yeshu to show him an appropriate verse to give Charan for this occasion. As he spoke the verse to Charan that morning, Charan listened intently. Charan would memorize this verse and carry it with him from this day forward.

As the three men came up out of the water, Arun took a garland of orange and yellow marigold flowers and placed it around Charan's neck.

Then the three moved to a quieter place farther from the water and sat down to have *Mahaprasad* together. According to Jay, *prasad* literally means "grace." Hindus use the word to refer to the food they eat after puja. The word *maha* means "great." By using maha with prasad, the Hindu believers in Jesus signify that this prasad they are eating is different from the normal prasad eaten at puja times. The Lord's Supper becomes "The Great Grace" and commemorates Sadguru Yeshu's body offered for them on the cross.

As a reminder and a symbol of Sadguru Yeshu's sacrifice, Pradip held a coconut over a bowl and picked up a hammer. He spoke of how the roughness of the coconut reminds us of the rough cross that Sadguru Yeshu was placed on. He smacked the coconut firmly several times with the hammer. As he did so, he said, "This reminds us of the nails pounded into his body." As the coconut split and the juice drained out into the bowl, Pradip said, "This shows us how Sadguru Yeshu's blood flowed for us." He separated the coconut into two halves and showed the fruit inside to Charan and Arun. He explained that the whiteness of this fruit reminds us that Sadguru Yeshu cleanses us from our sins. He is the firstfruits of the resurrection.

Each man held a small piece of roti, Indian flat bread, as Pradip read a few Bible verses about the Lord's Supper. They ate the bread and then each took a sip of the coconut juice.

Charan found the whole ceremony very meaningful. He said, "I feel so good, so free."

Before I left for the airport, Arun showed me a picture he had taken of Charan that morning. The photo showed a beaming boy with flowers around his neck and the rising sun gleaming off the water behind him.

I thought of how differently I'd come to see familiar practices during my visit to India. This baptism. A communion service. Church. Bible teaching. Worship songs. When I left India, I realized these familiar concepts still carried the same core meaning as before, but now I had seen them in almost completely different forms. What kinds of doors might these new forms open up?

I wondered if my journey to the Muslim world would open my eyes in even more new ways.

4

The Jamaat

"It's been a really clear road, being a weekday," said Cal shortly
after two oncoming trucks, side-by-side, pulled out tó pass a bus,
scattering pedestrians and bicyclists. Cal and I were heading as
rapidly as possible along this two-lane road in Bangladesh. We
had a tight schedule, which included a boat to catch and a *jamaat*
to attend.

Cal, after having spent fifteen years in Bangladesh, planned to
leave the country soon. He and his wife and children intended to
move back to their home country where Cal could finish his PhD.
He had graciously offered to take me along as he paid one last visit
to friends in various parts of the nation.

Some of Cal's friends were followers of Jesus who still called
themselves Muslims. I had come to Bangladesh because this nation
has, by some estimates, the most followers of Jesus from a Muslim
background of any country on earth. This makes Bangladesh one
of the best nations to get a glimpse of what it looks like to follow
Jesus within the culture of Islam.

As we made our way along the road, we saw water everywhere. One of Bangladesh's periodic floods was just subsiding. We crossed over muddy rivers and passed pond-like fields dotted with vibrant green rice plants.

Although nine in ten Bangladeshis follow the Islamic faith, the country has a sizeable minority of Hindus—9 percent. Christians represent only 0.66 percent of the population, but the number of believers in Christ has been growing faster than that of the general population for the last fifty years.[1]

No one knows for sure the total number of Muslim-background followers of Jesus in Bangladesh. Cal gave me what he considered a conservative estimate of two hundred thousand. *Operation World* reports "tens of thousands" of believers from a Muslim background, some of whom have come to faith through "Jesus mosques."[2]

As we talked in the back of the taxi, Cal made a surprising claim about what set the stage for so many Muslims to believe in Jesus. Cal said in his opinion there were two foundational events. One was the translation in 1980 of the Bible into the common language of the Muslim community in Bangladesh. The other was the Bangla translation in the early 1980s of the Qur'an.

It was fairly easy to understand Cal's first point. The Kitab, or Musalmani Bangla translation of the Bible, made God's Word suddenly more accessible to Muslims across Bangladesh. In the Bangla language, Hindus and Muslims use different words for the same thing. For "water," for example, Muslims would say "*pani*" and Hindus would say "*jol*." The Kitab used these ordinary Muslim words as well as some religious Muslim words, such as "Allah" for God.

The translators of the Kitab faced some resistance to their approach. The use of the word "Allah" still bothers some critics, who don't think believers in Christ should use this word for God. They claim the word "Allah" comes from a pagan background and the Allah of the Qur'an does not have the same attributes as the God of the Bible.

Proponents of the use of the word "Allah" for God point to the fact that millions of Christians in Indonesia, Egypt, and Syria use "Allah" to refer to God. They also point out that Bible translators in tribal areas routinely use the tribal word for high God to refer to Yahweh. In Bangladesh, for example, the Santal people, who number 628,000 and have responded in great numbers to the gospel, use their word "Thakur Jiu" or "Genuine God" for the God of the Bible. As for the God of the Qur'an being incompatible with the God of the Bible, that hasn't been the perception of many Muslims who have decided to follow Christ. "People will say, 'Before I knew about Allah; now I know Him. Before He was more distant. Now He's closer,'" Cal told me.

As the translators of the Kitab used "Allah" and other words from the Muslim vocabulary, they made God's Word more accessible to Muslims in Bangladesh. But what about the Bangla translation of the Qur'an? Wouldn't that hinder, rather than help, the message about Christ?

Not according to Cal. He said the Qur'an can lead readers to the Bible. He told me that most of the Bengalis he's met do not understand the Qur'an. They can recite it in Arabic, but often they don't understand the words they are saying. "They know maybe the vague story, but they don't know the messages and meaning of it," Cal said.

With a Bangla translation of the Qur'an, believers in Jesus can now point out those parts of the Qur'an that their friends and family may have never considered before. For instance, several times Muhammad encourages his followers to read the other holy books: the Tawrat (Old Testament), Zabur (Psalms), and Injil (the gospel revealed to Jesus, generally assumed to be the New Testament).[3] In addition, the Qur'an actually instructs readers to consult those who read the Bible. Surah 10:94 says, "If you were in doubt as to what We have revealed to you, then ask those who have been reading the Book from the Lord."[4]

In addition, the Qur'an often speaks of Jesus in a reverent way. The book includes two accounts of the birth of the man called

Isa.[5] The Qur'an gives Isa the title "Messiah" and describes Jesus as a "Word of God" and "Spirit of God."[6]

Many experts on the Muslim world have come to see the value of the Qur'an as a beginning point to introduce Muslims to the subject of Jesus. "It is widely known that many Muslims have come to Christ by first being pointed to Him by the Qur'an," wrote author and speaker Don McCurry.[7]

The Mob

We pulled up at a compound of steel-roofed dwellings. An L-shaped main house formed a courtyard ringed by eucalyptus trees. The smooth dirt yard had been neatly swept. In that peaceful place, it was hard to imagine the riot Cal's friends had been subjected to.

We greeted Akash, a quiet man with a neatly trimmed moustache. He was wearing a peach-colored shirt with pens sticking out of the pocket. Like many of the men we met, he was also wearing the lungi wrap. He showed us inside his house and offered Cal and me wooden chairs by the bed. After I sat down, and while Cal conversed with the men in Bangla, I looked around and noticed the bed. It consisted of a wooden frame with a plywood top, which was covered by a hard reed mat and floral-print sheets. I must be a soft American, I thought, because that looks too uncomfortable to sleep on.

Akash and another man, who I learned was Akash's brother, both sat down opposite us. Apparently the room where we were sitting also served as the meeting place for about thirteen believers in Isa. In the early '90s, a man came to Akash's village and handed out leaflets. This man worked with an organization I heard about repeatedly during my time in Bangladesh. The group helped pioneer a whole movement of fellowships of Jesus with an Islamic-style identity. They called their gatherings *jamaats*. The word "jamaat" means "community" in Arabic. In a spiritual sense, Muslims use this word to describe religious fellowship groups.

This initial organization, which I'll call "J Group," was started by a Bangladeshi soldier. I didn't find out how he came to faith in Jesus, but I learned that afterward he stayed within his Muslim culture. Though he kept his Muslim cultural identity, he also mingled with Christians. This man was a bold, dynamic evangelist and quickly led others to faith in Isa. Many of these first believers experienced dramatic dreams or healings.

Akash and his cousin wrote to the address on the J Group leaflet. "Nice books came through the mail," Akash remembered. Akash and his cousin read the New Testament and compared it with the Qur'an. "I learned more about the prophet Isa," recalled Akash. Eventually Akash and his cousin met with J Group leadership, decided to follow Isa, and were baptized. They were the first from their village to ever take this step.

Before long, word got out. A man with a loudspeaker stood by the school and called together a crowd, which grew to a mob of five thousand. The man claimed Akash and his cousin were reading the New Testament.

"I was really scared," Akash remembered.

People in the crowd were shouting, "Beat them! Beat them!" as the two young men were led to the front. Akash's cousin tried to address the crowd. He started, "In the name of Allah . . . " but was shouted down.

A couple of the village leaders said, "Don't do this," and took Akash and his cousin to see the head official. This official kept them in his office away from the angry crowd outside. He asked the two men what they believed. As Akash explained their faith starting from the Qur'an, Akash said he sensed the presence of God and the fear left him.

Finally, the mob dispersed, and Akash and his cousin went home in the midst of an uneasy state of tension with their community. Now, eight years later, that tension seemed to still linger.

I asked how the surrounding community now perceives them. "They somehow think it's a Christian group," Akash said, "but they don't say it. Somehow it's different and somehow it's the same, and they don't know how to express it."

The jamaat, composed of Akash's friends and relatives, meets on Sunday. They read the Bible, not the Qur'an. They don't sing. They pray together, but not in the *salat* style of Muslim prostration. Some of the jamaat members have gotten baptized. A few of the group still go to the mosque.

Periodically resistance to the jamaat flares up from villagers. Akash said when that happens, they pray as a group for protection.

As we drove on from Akash's house, I told Cal that some people say believers in Jesus in Islamic areas call themselves Muslims to avoid persecution. "If somebody said that to me seriously," Cal replied, "I would just laugh at them. They're not trying to avoid persecution because they can't. Every one of them goes through it. What they are trying to do is to stay in their heritage."

The Creed

For Akash and other believers, "Muslim" is just the word they've always called themselves. It refers not only to their beliefs but to their whole culture. They haven't left that culture and they say the belief they have come to is one that the Qur'an itself pointed them to. But to Christian analysts in various parts of the world, retaining this word "Muslim" has become an intensely debated issue.

Proponents argue that the word means "those who have submitted to God." Isn't submission to God a good posture for any believer in Jesus? Critics say yes, but that's not the way the average Muslim understands the word. To most followers of Islam, "Muslim" means a person who believes the Qur'an was divinely inspired and given to Muhammad, God's messenger. If people don't genuinely believe this doctrine, these critics say, they are deceiving others if they call themselves Muslim.

This issue is closely related to a second concern, the saying of the creed, or the *Shahada*: "I bear witness that 'There is no deity but God;' I bear witness that 'Muhammad is the messenger of God.'" This practice of saying the creed is one of the Five Pillars of the Islamic faith. Simply saying the Shahada one time, with sincere conviction, is all that is necessary to become a Muslim.[8] Can a believer in Isa still say Muhammad is God's messenger?

Some say "Yes." Muhammad gave them the Qur'an. In the Qur'an, they heard about Isa and learned about the other holy books. It was through these books (the Bible) that they came to faith.[9]

Others say "Yes, but." Yes, but they qualify the creed. "There is no deity but Allah and Isa is the Straight Path." Or yes, but maybe believers won't be able to say the Shahada in good conscience as they grow in faith.

Cal said that in Bangladesh, believers who do say the creed seem to qualify it.

"What about the other practices," I asked Cal, "the other pillars of Islam? In Bangladesh, do believers keep doing everything the same? Do they pray five times a day, fast during Ramadan, give alms, even take pilgrimages to Mecca?"

According to Cal, Akash's group was fairly typical regarding mosque attendance and use of the Qur'an. I was curious why they didn't sing at their jamaat. Cal said, "A large part of Islam doesn't like singing in religious worship. And it tends to identify conversion."

As for fasting, Cal said some believers still fast. In the Muslim community of Bangladesh as a whole, Cal observed that some Muslims diligently keep the fast every day, including not drinking during daylight hours even if they labor in the hot sun outside. But many Muslims fast diligently only at the beginning and end of Ramadan.

Regarding praying five times a day, a few believers in Isa still do that, he said, but many people in the wider Islamic community, particularly in rural areas, do not practice these daily prayers.

It was interesting to me how relaxed Akash's attitude was about the salat, or ritual Muslim prayer. I read one critic of Muslim believers in Jesus who said that maintaining traditions like the salat only allows empty legalism to remain in the believer's life. "There is an inextricable linking of works for salvation with a worship focusing on details, externals, ritual movements, holy words and proper washings," he wrote.[10] On the other hand, I also read about the experience of a man who said after he began to follow Isa, the salat took on new meaning. "These times of prayer and worship are no longer an obligation but a joyful time with my Savior," he stated.[11]

Where Akash lived in rural Bangladesh, it seemed they didn't feel any legalistic compulsion about this matter one way or the other. He and his jamaat could leave the issue of the salat as a personal choice, and their position on this could still fit roughly within the common practice of Muslims in their area.

The pilgrimage to Mecca also wasn't an issue for believers in Bangladesh, Cal said. It's an optional practice anyway, and one most Bangladeshis can't afford.

The Evangelist

The day after our visit to Akash, Cal and I hit the road again, this time to catch a boat. We were headed to a very remote place. In the area we planned to visit across the river, Cal said as far as he knew there had never been any Christians living there nor any ongoing Christian ministry. He said there might be a hundred Muslim followers of Jesus living in this area but guessed that he might be the only foreigner who even knew they were there.

At the river, we walked down the earthen bank. Our vessel was a forty-foot, sharp-prowed wooden boat about six feet wide. A curved covering of woven reeds spanned the center. We clambered aboard and a young man used a pole to push us away from shore as another man got the engine going. It thumped away, spewing steam, and we were off.

This river, one of the waterways the Ganges empties into, was so wide I could only faintly see the other shore in the distance. A boat similar to ours passed us, loaded with more than thirty people, some of them sitting on a mound of goods piled in the middle. In their wake, I could see clusters of water hyacinths floating on the current.

Along with Cal and me in our boat, there were only two fellow travelers. One of them, Rajib, planned to take us with him to visit his home. Rajib, wearing a blue shirt, black trousers, and sandals, smiled from under the canopy as I put my day pack under cover. Even resting there, Rajib, a middle-aged man with glasses and a moustache, looked focused and intense.

Like Akash, he had come to faith in Jesus through the literature of J Group. Rajib became the first follower of Jesus in his whole area. Just to get fellowship, he would travel all the way across the river and many miles beyond that to visit Tripon, a leader in J Group.

Rajib told many people about his beliefs. The community responded forcefully. At one point, an angry crowd surrounded the compound where he and his family lived. They wouldn't let anyone in or out. Cal said, "It was a siege, like a war."

The village would not provide any of his family with jobs, and Rajib couldn't grow enough on his land to survive. Later Rajib admitted that sometimes his family couldn't eat for three days in a row because they were so poor.

Cal asked, "Why did your family side with you?"

"Because it's right," Rajib responded.

"Then why don't more people believe it?" Cal inquired.

"Our history is to follow the Qur'an and follow Muhammad," Rajib explained. "To change is to move outside history and community. That's who we are, what we do." Now, though, he said, "Just with the Qur'an we can show what is right, who Jesus is."

As we reached the other shore, a dozen boys were jumping into the muddy water. They had to make way for our boat to pull in.

As we walked up the bank, four men came to greet Rajib and Cal. They took us to four parked motorcycles, which we got on. We all headed down the sandy lane that led away from the river.

Eventually we pulled into a compound of about five steel-clad buildings. A black sign announced the name of a social service organization. Cal and I met more people and then were ushered into an office. A man, who seemed to be the director, sat behind a desk that was draped in white cloth on which snacks had been laid out. Cal, Rajib, and I took our places on blue plastic chairs near the director. About ten other men crowded into the room, sitting on chairs that lined the aqua walls.

The director, Zahir, seemed just as intense as Rajib. A fortyish man wearing a white checked shirt, he obviously enjoyed being in charge, and he seemed to be thinking ahead all the time.

After explaining the agricultural and medical work of his organization, Zahir told us about his initial encounters with Rajib. He didn't like it at first that Rajib kept trying to get him to read the Bible. But finally he agreed to at least look at some verses in the Qur'an. That made him curious about what the Kitab, the Muslim-language Bible, had to say. He compared the two books. He read the stories about Jesus. He reflected on the virgin birth of Jesus. He became aware that "He is the most honorable. As we see that, we need to learn to follow Him."

Zahir, with Rajib's encouragement, did just that. He decided to follow Jesus. Then he began sharing his faith with other members of the organization. Now, of the 125 employees, fifty have become believers. Rajib leads a jamaat in this building every Sunday. About fifty people attend. Also Rajib told us about four more jamaats, including one that meets at his home.

That's where we headed late in the day after several more meetings in town. Again we rode on the back of motorcycles. The pinks and oranges of the sunset glistened in the watery fields.

It was after dark when we stopped at Rajib's farm. I could just make out three or four small buildings with steel roofs and jute walls.

One of Rajib's family members showed me to my room. I had been given a nice Bengali-style bed, with wooden frame, plywood top, reed mat, and clean sheet. I would have a chance to find out if I really could sleep on such a bed after all.

The next morning, after I stiffly got up and had breakfast, Rajib barked out orders to his clan and called for a meeting. A group of about nineteen people gathered. The men and women sat on different sides of the room. Cal taught from the Gospel of Mark.

While Cal spoke, a sheep wandered by, nuzzling the steps. I could hear boys splashing in the water nearby. I followed their voices and then spotted them in the rice field. The watery pasture and the river beyond it reflected a cloud-strewn sky. Across the river, on an elevated path under the trees, two women in saris walked by, bright splashes of red and yellow against the green and blue.

The Kitchen Jamaat

Back on the other side of the river, on a Friday afternoon, Cal and I finally arrived at Tripon's jamaat. To get there, our car wound around groups of men talking after prayers at the mosque. Then we stopped at a three-story concrete building, walked through a gate, took off our shoes, and met Tripon. A tall, graying man, Tripon ushered us into his office to visit while we waited for the jamaat members to arrive. We sat on a little couch by a green file cabinet.

I found out that we had entered Tripon's apartment. He came to this town in the '90s purposely to start a jamaat. He was not aware of any believers in this area before he came.

Tripon had grown up in a devout Muslim family. In his early teens, a foreign Christian gave him a copy of the Injil, the New Testament. He spent hours comparing it to the Qur'an and found himself increasingly impressed by the teaching of the Injil and drawn to the person of Isa.

Eventually he committed himself to follow Isa as his Savior. He joined a Christian agency and worked for them in translation. Then he met the founder of J Group and served as an evangelist and teacher with them for nearly ten years. When he arrived in this town, he had just left J Group.

As Cal and I talked with Tripon in the office, people started coming by in the hallway outside. One thin man, carrying a red motorcycle helmet, looked in and smiled at us. Another, a fit, balding man with a neatly trimmed beard, came in and greeted us warmly. That, I found out, was Arif, Tripon's landlord.

Arif was one of the first people to express interest in Tripon's faith in Isa. As an influential man in the community, Arif faced tremendous opposition when he also confessed that Isa was his Savior. He was beaten, tied up, and put in prison. His wife, horrified at this change in her husband, also criticized him. Today Arif has become Tripon's right-hand man in leading the jamaat. His wife also has chosen to follow Isa. This fellowship of believers has grown to nearly fifty. Through this jamaat, two other groups have formed as well.

Cal said the believers in Tripon's jamaat are known in the community as "Isa-e." To Muslims in the community, Cal explained, the Isa-e term probably means something new, something connected to Christianity but different.

Tripon used the ambiguity of the group's identity to help him counsel new believers. Cal told me he heard Tripon advise one young man to stop going to the mosque. Tripon was concerned about the influence mosque leaders and Muslim practices, such as saying the creed, were having on this man. To another young man, Tripon said, "Don't break with your parents. Go to the mosque."

For this man, going to the mosque maintained his family relationships at a crucial time.

In spite of their Christian-influenced identity, Tripon and Arif had built good relationships throughout the town. For Christmas and Easter, they would invite people to come and join them for a celebration. For Christmas, which is a national holiday, they arranged for a vehicle with a loudspeaker to drive around the town announcing the event. On a typical Christmas, more than two hundred people show up to their party. Even district commissioners attend the celebration, which is a full-day event held on the flat roof of Arif's building. They string up lights, sing songs, preach from the Bible, and serve lunch. They offer tracts and books. Visitors come and go.

Now new believers do not receive the abuse that Tripon and Arif endured. As town members have seen the lives of the believers in the jamaat, they have softened their attitudes. "Now they see that Isa-e is also good," Cal said. "It's a way that leads to salvation."

In fact, Cal said he heard about a young man who had attended the jamaat and finally got up the courage to tell his parents. They said, "Oh, thank Allah! We knew you weren't happy before. This is a good group." That wasn't the reaction the young man expected! Cal explained, "Parents know there are bad groups around. Their son could have gotten involved in something occult or immoral. Isa-e has a reputation for hospitality, openness, and good works."

Cal admitted this isn't a typical response for new believers in other groups, but Tripon's group, as one of the more influential jamaats in the nation, does show how community attitudes can change.

It was now time for the meeting to begin. We made our way down the hallway, past a sink, and into the dining room. The table had been removed and a carpet laid down that covered most of the floor. In the center rested a stack of thick red Bibles and green songbooks. Men and boys sat crowded together on the floor. They looked up and smiled at us as we picked our way through the crowd to the spot where Tripon motioned for us to sit.

At one edge of the room was a small bed covered in a red sheet. That, apparently, was the seat of honor for Cal, Arif, another man, and me. Next to us was a fridge, then the cooking room, and then a bedroom with open door. In this bedroom, the women and girls, dressed in yellow, orange, and green saris with shawls over their heads, sat on the bed and the floor and looked through the doorway at us. In keeping with Muslim culture, they participated in worship separately from the men.

The bed where we sat was behind Tripon, so I could look into the upturned faces in front of me. One man with glasses and a white beard held on his lap a boy of about eight, wearing a blue shirt. I counted thirty-four males in total. Tripon stood at a wooden pulpit just in front of the little bed and began the meeting. A fan whirred over his head and a gecko crawled down the wall as he spoke.

He began with a prayer. He held his hands out in front of him, palms up, and prayed with his eyes open. As he prayed, some of the men in front of me also turned their palms upward and lifted their hands slightly.

Tripon asked the group to read with him from the songbook. The stack of green books disappeared as the books were passed around the room. After the reading, he asked for song suggestions. They sang two songs, Bangladeshi-style tunes, without instruments. They sang earnestly. I watched an older man who had a wispy white goatee. He wore a white kurta and a white lungi. Some of his teeth were missing. He sang with enthusiasm, gesturing with one hand in front of him, fingers pressed together, as his other hand held the songbook.

After the singing, the green books came back to their stack and the Bibles were passed out. Arif prayed. Then Tripon began to preach.

I looked at the faces in front of me. The boy in the blue shirt had fallen asleep. All the others gave Tripon their rapt attention.

Tripon spoke about Paul's encounter with Jesus on the road to Damascus. "Paul was blind and then he didn't see the same," Tripon said. "Isn't that the same for us? We don't look at the world in the same way."

As I left Bangladesh, I didn't see the same way either. I had now begun to discern how Muslims could follow Jesus in their own cultural style. I had been inspired by believers who endured persecution and still remained bold to speak about their faith. I had seen the power of the Bible to completely change the direction of people's lives. I felt encouraged at the flexibility I saw regarding identity—many followers of Jesus would use the term "Christian" at times, "Muslim" at other times, and something in between, like "Isa-e," as well. They related both to the Christian community and the Muslim community. I could picture them now, bowing to the floor, or lifting hands in prayer.

What I couldn't picture so well was what a disciple of Jesus might look like in a Buddhist culture. How could a person retain their customs when their culture doesn't believe in a creator God?

My encounter with a monk in Thailand gave me a clue.

5

The Monk

It was nearing midnight as I and the other groggy travelers from my plane walked into the Bangkok airport and queued up for an escalator. Ahead of me a Thai man herded his children and luggage, trying to get the whole family moving in the right direction. As I paused behind the man, I noticed the peaceful, sleeping face of his little daughter. He held her against his chest and her head rested on his shoulder.

As I stood there, I pondered a couple of things. Would this girl ever meet a Christian in her entire life? If she did, would she have any inkling that these strange beliefs could be true?

I was full of questions because I was having a hard time imagining what faith in Christ could look like within a Buddhist country like this one. I had come here to get answers, but I honestly couldn't imagine what these answers might be. I had heard about a monk who followed Jesus and stayed within his Buddhist culture. I had even heard about groups of believers calling themselves "New Buddhists." But how could Buddhist practices and a biblical worldview possibly fit together?

Grandma's Dance

I didn't have to wait long to find out. The next day I traveled across Bangkok to meet a Thai couple, Inchai and Ruth Srisuwan. I found them in a classroom-sized room ringed with traditional-looking musical instruments. We sat at a long table and they told me their story.

After they came to faith in Christ, Inchai and Ruth wanted to serve others with their musical skills. As a first step, they studied Western church music. When they graduated, they went out to Isaan in Northeast Thailand and joined a team of people working with villagers there. The rural men and women struggled to learn the hymns that Inchai and Ruth taught them.

Then one day as the believers sat together on straw mats and talked about the Bible, an elderly woman stood up and walked into the middle of the circle. She began to dance. She made small, precise steps in the Isaan style and waved her thin arms back and forth in rhythm.

A young person in the group said, "Grandma, sit down! What do you think you're doing?"

Without any pause in her dance, she replied, "You don't tell your old grandma to sit down. I'm ninety years old and I'm just thanking the Lord that you're here."

From then on, the little groups of believers began to incorporate dance into their worship. Inchai and Ruth felt inspired to learn the Isaan traditional music. One of the first instruments Inchai tackled was a bamboo mouth organ called the *khaen*. He explained that in every village at least one person would own a khaen and would know how to play it. A man might learn from his brother or a son from his grandfather. Not only did Inchai study how to play the khaen, but he also learned how to make them.

As Ruth tried to describe the sound of the khaen, Inchai got up and said, "As you talk, I will play it for you."

He picked up a large instrument that had a double row of reeds ranging from about three feet to two feet in length. He held it in the center with both hands. As he played, a full, organ-like sound came out.

He played an upbeat song. Before long, Ruth stood up and moved next to her husband. She had become the dance instructor for the groups. A pretty, middle-aged woman with hair pulled back and glasses, she was wearing a red and yellow shirt with an ankle-length tiger-print skirt. She began to sing in a clear voice. She also made small steps with her feet and swayed as she gracefully moved her arms. As she did so, she made careful shapes with her fingers. Sometimes a finger might touch her thumb. Sometimes her fingers would bend backwards and spread out.

They told me that during harvesttime they would walk out to the fields with their friends. In midafternoon, people would gather under a tree. The villagers would bring sticky rice with them to the field and then look for mushrooms, frogs, or vegetables to cook. Someone would play the khaen, the people would dance, they would discuss the Bible together, and then they would all share the meal.

Inchai and Ruth said they would stay in a community long enough to train a Bible leader, a musician, and a song leader and then they would move on to a new place. Now they had relocated to Bangkok to work with the residents of a very poor community. They walked with me to a small home and introduced me to some of the families.

Inchai and Ruth have incorporated many aspects of Thai culture into their gatherings. Back at their office, Ruth picked up a ten-inch-long piece of braided yellow yarn. She told me in Isaan culture a host might tie a string on a guest's wrist as a way "to show love or care." She demonstrated by tying the string on me.

She said they use string tying in this community as well as a water ceremony that is part of *Songkran*, Thai New Year. They also teach Thai music and dance. Their office held a variety of the instruments they use—drums of many sizes, something like a xylophone, and a kind of cello with only two strings.

They said at first Christians resisted the use of the khaen. "They said the khaen is Buddhist," Inchai recalled. "But it doesn't belong to Buddhists. It belongs to God. God gave the knowledge to the people. He gave the ability to make good sounds. Why not use it?"

Inchai and Ruth have joined a growing number of Christ-followers who seek to live out their faith in Buddhist style. They use festivals, movements, sounds, and customs from Buddhist culture.

To get an idea how far this kind of fusion of Christian faith and Buddhist culture could go, it helps to journey back in time to a community that emerged in China more than thirteen hundred years ago.

Discovering the Religion of Light

It all began in 635 AD when Christian emissaries of the Church of the East, often called the Nestorian Church, reached China. The Chinese emperor greeted this little band of messengers kindly. He welcomed this new teaching as he also had welcomed Buddhist teachers coming from India. He ordered Bishop Aloben and his companions to translate their writings into the Chinese language. He also sponsored the building of monasteries in dozens of cities.

With the help of a Chinese man named Jingjing, Aloben and the others translated their documents not only into the language but also into the way of thinking of the Chinese people. Eventually Chinese believers, perhaps Jingjing himself, wrote worship poetry of their own.

We know this story because in 1625 Chinese workmen digging a grave in the countryside near Xian discovered an enormous stone slab. This carved stone, called a stele, told the story of a new religion in China, the Religion of Light.

Three hundred years later, explorers stumbled onto a cave full of ancient treasures. They uncovered scrolls, artifacts, and paintings dating from the fifth to eleventh centuries. Together with the stone stele, these documents, called sutras, provide a tantalizing glimpse into a faith that dramatically synthesized Christian teachings with Buddhist and Taoist worldviews.

Restoration of the original painting, which is now in the British Museum. Used by permission of Martin Palmer. Copyright 2001 by Martin Palmer.

Author Martin Palmer, who wrote a bestselling book describing these findings, called this expression of the Christian faith "one of the most radical and experimental of all Churches ever to have existed."[1]

As the Religion of Light took shape, it formed unique and fascinating communities. They banned slavery and discouraged the taking of any life. As a result, they became officially vegetarian.

One of the unearthed paintings provides an intriguing insight into their style of worship. It was painted on a frail silk banner. The painting shows a frontal view of a man with a thin moustache, dressed in robes, and wearing a crown-like headdress and necklace and bracelets. In his left hand he holds a staff. He gestures with his right arm, the hand bent backward, palm facing forward, with his second finger touching his thumb.

Palmer surmises this could be a painting of a *bodhisattva*, a person on the path to Buddhahood, except there are three crosses in the painting: one on the headdress, one on the staff, and one on the necklace. Palmer guesses this picture portrays a Christian saint, or maybe Jesus Himself.

In Buddhist paintings, wrote Palmer, the hand position, or mudra, depicted in this painting symbolizes teaching. If the painter ascribed meaning to this hand position, Palmer guesses the believers in China also may have used their hands in worship. "We can picture members of the Church in China standing, arms raised, using mudra hand gestures to signify different aspects of the service or meaning in the liturgy."[2]

To read the writings of the Religion of Light, recorded in the sutra scrolls and on the stone stele, is to read descriptions of Christian concepts in totally new words. For example, the Stone Sutra states:

> In the beginning was the natural constant, the true stillness of the Origin, and the primordial void of the Most High. Then, the spirit of the void emerged as the Most High Lord, moving in mysterious ways to enlighten the holy ones. He is Joshua, my True Lord of the Void, who embodies the three subtle and wondrous bodies,

and who was condemned to the cross so that the people of the four directions can be saved.[3]

The text on the stone uses Buddhist imagery to explain the significance of what Christ has done: "He set afloat the raft of salvation and compassion so that we can use it to ascend to the palace of light and be united with the spirit."[4]

Also the sutras do not shy away from using Buddhist concepts to describe salvation. For example, through Christ, God saves us from karma. "God suffered terrible woes so that all should be freed from karma, for nobody is beyond the reach of the Buddha principle."[5]

At times the sutras beautifully describe the release God offers humanity from the terrible weight of earning enough merit:

> Then the Compassionate Knowing One came like the close
> relative
> And taught them with skill and sincerity so they knew
> That He is the scaling ladder and the steps cut in stone
> By which they can find the true Way, freed of their weight
> forever.[6]

The sutras also give a glimpse into the heart of a worshiping community:

> The highest skies are in love with You.
> The great Earth opens its palms in peace.
> Our truest being is anchored in Your Purity.
> You are Allaha: Compassionate Father of the Three.
> Everything praises you, sounding its true note.
> All the Enlightened chant praises—
> Every being takes its refuge in You
> And the light of Your Holy Compassion frees us all.
> Beyond knowing, beyond words
> You are the truth, steadfast for all time.
> Compassionate Father, Radiant Son,
> Pure Wind King—three in one.[7]

As beautiful as the sutras can be, there are also some parts that seem to stray away from core biblical teaching. One mentions that the emperor got his position because of his deeds in former lives.[8] Another says "The Messiah is not the Honored One."[9] The sutras do have confusing and disturbing parts.

The Religion of Light seems to have faded away starting in 845. In that year, the emperor ordered all monks—Buddhist, Taoist, and Nestorian—to "return to the world."[10] At this time, tens of thousands of people followed the Religion of Light.[11] It's not clear why this Christian movement dwindled after the emperor ended his support of the monks. Perhaps if there had been more of an effort at Bible translation, these groups of believers might have thrived even after this setback.

Whatever the reason for the untimely end of the Religion of Light, the two hundred years of its existence produced remarkable innovation. In considering the practices of the Religion of Light, Palmer found inspiration for the followers of Christ today. "As Christians slowly and tentatively feel their way toward a more mature relationship with other faiths and cultures, the Jesus Sutras stand as a beacon showing it has been done before."[12]

A Monk Leaves the Forest

Two days after my visit with Inchai and Ruth, I found myself on the back of a motorcycle winding through another Thai city. My driver for this afternoon was none other than the monk I had been hearing about before coming to Thailand. Actually, Jao wasn't a monk anymore. Having recently left the *sangha*, the monastic community, he was studying to become a tour guide. He had agreed to show me a couple of temples.

We parked outside a large white building with an ornate red and gold roof. We walked up orange-tiled steps past carved dragons, slipped off our sandals, and entered the quiet interior. A middle-aged man wearing a yellow-orange robe was just finishing his talk to about twenty people who were sitting on plastic chairs. Off to the side, a group of boys dressed like the older monk sat on the floor with their hands clasped in front of them. The face of one of the younger children, who seemed no more than twelve years old, caught my eye. I imagined Jao sitting in a place like this many years before.

When he was thirteen, Jao's parents had sent him off to a temple in the forest to become a monk. Jao explained that although most Thai young men choose to spend only three months or so as monks when they reach their early twenties, other boys come to the temple much younger and spend the rest of their childhood there.

For Jao, the journey by bus from his home to the temple took ten hours. He went back to visit his family only once a year. As a monk, Jao had to observe strict rules, such as not to touch women, even his own mother, and not to kill any living thing. He also went out in the mornings with a big alms bowl to receive gifts of food.

I asked him if it was a hard decision to leave the monastery. He said, "Yes, it was very difficult." As a monk, he said, you have a place to sleep and food to eat and clothes to wear. He also had money to cover his other expenses. These funds came from a Thai lady who sponsored him. She didn't have any male children of her own who could become monks, so she sent him money even after she moved to the United States. She had become Jao's benefactor as a way to earn merit. This was how the Buddha envisioned it. The monks earn merit by their religious service. The laypeople earn merit by supporting the monks.[13]

When Jao left his monastic forest home, the monastery gave him a little money and some clothes. He was grateful to find a job as a waiter. Today, dressed in a gray T-shirt, jeans, and sandals, carrying a small backpack, he looked like a college student, which is what he was. He had undergone quite a change from the boy with a shaved head and orange robes. But Jao's change on the outside was not as great as the change on the inside.

I had heard this part of the story from Jao's friend, Mark. Soon after Mark, Emily, and their three children moved to Thailand, they met Jao. As they got to know Jao better, they wondered how to speak to him about his beliefs and how to communicate their own faith. One day Mark's three-year-old daughter suggested they pray for Jao to have a dream. After they prayed, Jao did have a series of dreams in which Jesus appeared to him. These dreams led him to faith in Jesus as his Savior.

He didn't become a Christian though. He wanted to maintain his friendships and relationships in the Buddhist community. He didn't want to leave his Buddhist culture and join the Christian culture. He would still go and visit friends at a Buddhist temple and stay there overnight. He also met regularly with Mark to discuss the Bible and his faith. "He's got this circle of friends around him that he's slowly prompting to consider Jesus in their context," Mark told me.

Although he doesn't attend a Christian church, Jao considers Christians his sisters and brothers in Christ. He hopes to find friends who follow Christ within his own culture. Mark told me one of the most common derogatory names Thais call Christians is *luksit farang*, which means "disciple of a foreigner."

Jao will pray fervently sitting cross-legged and speaking in his native Isaan language. He also retains an awareness of the spirit world. One night he stayed at a friend's house and had a dream that featured members of his friend's family. In the morning, he told his hosts the dream. They said the dream contained accurate details about the family, facts he couldn't have known. The family attributed the dream to the local spirit. They told Jao they wanted him to come with them to see the local spiritist. Jao went along and watched them do their rituals. He told Mark, "I don't have a problem with that. It's very possible that dream came from that spirit. That doesn't make me one who wished for such a dream."

Festivals and Dramas

Like Jao, many other believers in Thailand and neighboring countries now follow Jesus within their Buddhist culture. Paul DeNeui, a professor who spent eighteen years in Thailand, wrote about his encounters with Buddhist-background believers all across the C-Scale.

In Thailand, many join Western-style C1 or C2 churches, but some fellowships fit the C3 model, where they worship in a more traditionally Thai style. They take off their shoes and sit on mats. They might use *Satoo*, a Pali word for "so be it," in place of "Amen."[14]

Some fellowships fit the C4 description. They avoid the label "Christian" and instead call themselves by names such as "Child of God," or "Church of the Grace of God." They give food to monks in the name of Jesus and incorporate rituals like string tying, explaining that it has no magic power but it can help believers visualize the concept of the love of Christ.

Of these C4 fellowships, DeNeui wrote, "Many have stated it is the first time they feel they could follow Jesus and still remain a Thai."

A man named Joe, who works in Southeast Asia, told me stories about specific believers who choose to remain within their Buddhist culture. He said he knows a Thai woman who along with her coworkers has baptized more than fifteen thousand people near Bangkok. A small minority of these believers do not call themselves Christians but simply Buddhists. "She and her five trainees are too busy discipling and training new leaders to deal with the titles yet," Joe wrote.

Joe also reported that the network of churches in Isaan that Inchai and Ruth worked with has now grown to more than 330 churches. Joe said some of these believers do not call themselves Christians but instead use the phrase "Children of God." Another group of fellowships loosely connected to this movement call themselves "New Buddhists." These New Buddhists have baptized about 500 people according to Joe.

As Jao and I walked through the temple, we passed a room where three worshipers had knelt down before a seated monk. Smoke from incense wafted above their heads. The monk said some kind of chant and gave them each a piece of string to tie on their wrist.

Increasing numbers of Buddhist-background believers have been thinking not only about customs like string tying, but also about festivals.

One of these festivals is *Loi Krathong*, the Festival of Lights. After harvest, people give thanks to the god of the river, and they honor the Buddha with light. They construct a float from banana leaves or bread, add flowers, place a candle in the center, and then launch it on the river. They trust that the candle will carry away "all that the sender wanted to get rid of, including sin and wrongdoing."[15]

According to Ruth and Inchai, most Christians reject the festival entirely. Their church instead gives thanks to God for the rain by planting something during this festival. Author John Davis, while admitting this isn't an issue for him to resolve, wondered if the festival could be reinvested with new meaning "to declare the other Way of removing sins, the other Way of finding forgiveness."[16]

Davis, who lived in Thailand for thirty years, wrote that these festivals play a crucial role in Buddhist communities. The celebrations form an integral part of the life of the society. "Not only would a Buddhist feel lost in the cosmos without the religious significance of these ceremonies," Davis stated, "but he would also be lost socially."[17] He added that since the Christian church mainly reduces ceremonies to Sunday functions, this leaves a "colossal vacuum."[18] He concluded, "This may be one of the most important reasons why the gospel has not taken root in Buddhist countries."

In addition to experimenting with festivals and customs, some Christians have also used Buddhist-influenced art forms. The *Likay* folk drama, which combines singing, dancing, narration, and improvisational acting, draws large crowds in Thailand. Usually the stories feature a villain, a hero, and a couple of simpleminded comedians. Many of the performers dress in glittering costumes.

For decades the Christian Communications Institute of Payap University has used *Likay* in rural areas to communicate the gospel. Using the traditional bright costumes and exaggerated makeup, they perform in twenty-five villages each year. Their rich man in the Lazarus story commits all kinds of corruption, something the Thai audience can relate to. "But Lazarus learned that faith in Christ makes anyone a new person," says the troupe's brochure.[19]

Beyond the stories themselves, dressing the message in such a traditional style shows the gospel in Buddhist-like clothing. "Such performances serve to break down prejudices against Christianity, which is normally regarded as a Western foreign religion," reported John Davis.[20]

As I rode from the temple on the back of Jao's motorcycle, I knew he was trying to forge a new way for faith in his country, one that would look and feel Thai and not foreign. It was a lonely road. He still had not found a Thai fellowship to belong to. He told me, as we shouted to each other over the rush of wind, that he would like to see the day when more people in his country would read the stories of Jesus. They won't just read them as stories, he said, but they will think about the meaning.

I know Jao carried with him a picture. It's a photograph of a painting. Mark showed me a copy of it. He told me Jao carries it with him wherever he goes. Mark explained that the Buddhist culture is very visual, and this painting inspires Jao in his love for God. In the picture, a radiant, white-robed Jesus gestures to five men in the foreground. The men each come from a different ethnic group. There's an African, a Latino, an Anglo, and two Asians. They all seem to be praying, one pressing his hands together, two raising their arms, one kneeling, another bowing. Behind them, Jesus holds out His nail-pierced hands in welcome, beckoning them all to come.

As I rode along, the humid air buffeting my face, I realized I had found an unexpected richness in the customs, the language, and the festivals of Buddhist culture. I pictured the row of golden Buddha statues I had seen in one temple, each with different finger and body postures, and I thought of the power of visual symbolism. In my mind I heard again the drone of the khaen and saw Ruth's fingers form mudra hand positions, now used in worship of the Triune Creator God.

The images from my many journeys through Asia filled my imagination. I had already witnessed believers use a tremendous variety of movements, sounds, events, imagery, and vocabulary in their relationship with the God of the Bible. But I knew my voyage of discovery still wasn't finished. I also wanted to see how people from a tribal culture live out their faith in Jesus. For that, I knew I could simply go home, get on the highway, and drive.

6

The Powwow

The National Western Event Center in Denver, Colorado, seemed dark and quiet on this Sunday morning, the last day of the Thanksgiving Powwow. A few people readied items for display in booths near the big entrance doors. Soon the bleachers would fill with Native American dancers and their families.

Down below, in the center of the vast, indoor dirt arena, a light shone on a man tuning his guitar. He stood in front of sixteen white folding chairs arranged in rows. I looked for a stairway down to join him. By the time I got there, several others had already taken their seats. It was almost time for the Christian Indian Center's Sunday service to begin.

We sang some songs led by a man and a woman each playing a guitar. Another man played an Indian hand drum. One of the songs I recognized, but two others were new to me. They were both written by Jonathan Maracle, a Native American songwriter. It was a bit daunting to sing with fewer than a dozen people in that cavernous stadium. Our voices sounded feeble in all that space.

After an offering, a few members of the congregation mentioned prayer requests. Then Richard Silversmith preached a short sermon. As he spoke, I looked above him at the entry doors. Families had now begun to arrive. Some pulled small rolling suitcases. Others carefully carried garments that sparkled and tinkled. The men, women, and children made their way down into the empty bleachers.

Silversmith was talking about the irony of the Thanksgiving holiday. Most Americans like to remember the story of the first Thanksgiving. In 1621 the Pilgrims celebrated their first successful corn harvest. They had spent one year in the New World, and already half of the original 102 passengers on the *Mayflower* had died. If not for the help of friendly Native Americans, who taught them how to cultivate corn among other things, many more may have perished. Governor William Bradford called for a celebratory feast and invited the tiny colony's Native American allies to join them. In honor of this event, in 1863 President Abraham Lincoln declared Thanksgiving a national holiday.

Almost exactly one year later, on November 29, 1864, less than two hundred miles from where I sat in Denver, a group of volunteer Colorado militia led by Col. John Chivington silently approached a Native American settlement on the banks of Sand Creek. Although the Cheyenne and Arapaho tribes had camped there at the request of the governor of Colorado and although they were flying flags to indicate a peaceful camp, Chivington and his volunteers killed approximately two hundred people. Most of the victims were women, children, and the elderly.

One observer of the slaughter wrote to a friend later, "I tell you Ned it was hard to see little children on their knees have their brains beat out by men professing to be civilized."[1]

The day before our worship service, Silversmith had met with a small group of people on the steps of the Colorado capitol to commemorate what became known as the Sand Creek Massacre. Now Silversmith, of Navajo ancestry, spoke about the feelings that emerge for him as a Native American on Thanksgiving weekend. He spoke of the history of bloodshed that began with Cain and Abel. "How do we find hope?" he asked. "We look to God's guidance in our lives."

In the ugly history of whites and Natives in North America, many have questioned where to find hope and how to understand God. In 1890 a man dusted snow off the crumpled bodies at the scene of another massacre—the one at Wounded Knee, South Dakota. The man inspecting the bodies was a doctor, leading a team of a hundred civilians who were trying to find survivors.

Ohiyesa's Faith

The man was no ordinary doctor. He was born in a buffalo-hide tepee in 1858 near Redwood Falls, Minnesota. In his youth he was given the name Ohiyesa. Until the age of fifteen, he lived in the forests of southern Manitoba as a nomadic Sioux. He fully expected to live the rest of his days as a Sioux hunter and warrior. As he prepared to enter manhood, he planned to go on the warpath to avenge the death of his father, who had been captured by whites when Ohiyesa was only four years old.

But then one day his father walked into camp. He had escaped from his captors and now had finally found his family again.

His father said he had been doing a lot of thinking and had concluded that the Native American's best hope was to learn the white man's ways. "Above all, they have their Great Teacher, whom they call Jesus," Ohiyesa's father said, "and He taught them to pass on their wisdom and knowledge to other races. . . . The sooner we accept their mode of life and follow their teaching, the better it will be for us all."[2]

Ohiyesa went back with his father to the plot of land in South Dakota where his father was attempting to farm. Reluctantly the boy agreed to begin attending school. After a couple of difficult days trying to understand the strange language, Ohiyesa felt like giving up. He went where his grandmother had taught him to go in such times, into the forest. He sought the "Great Mystery," the Creator, in silence.

"When I came back," Ohiyesa wrote later, "my heart was strong. I desired to follow the new trail to the end."[3]

This unfamiliar trail took Ohiyesa from the tiny village school to a mission-run boarding school in Santee, Nebraska. From there he journeyed on to Beloit College in Wisconsin, then to Dartmouth College, and finally to medical school at Boston University. Ohiyesa's father, Many Lightnings, had taken the name Jacob Eastman. Ohiyesa named himself Charles.

Ohiyesa became known to the world as Charles Eastman. After a short medical career, he became a lobbyist in Washington for the Sioux tribe, worked for the YMCA establishing Christian fellowships among Native Americans throughout the western United States and Canada, and wrote eleven books. He became the foremost Native American spokesman of his day.

Eastman also could write with feeling both of his faith in Jesus and of the beliefs of the Sioux. Like most North American tribes, Eastman's Sioux tribe was monotheistic. A sense of the spiritual filled every aspect of life, Eastman recalled.

> Whenever, in the course of the daily hunt, the red hunter comes upon a scene that is strikingly beautiful and sublime—a black thundercloud with the rainbow's glowing arch above the mountain; a white waterfall in the heart of a green gorge; a vast prairie tinged with the blood-red of sunset—he pauses for an instant in the attitude of worship. He sees no need for setting apart one day in seven as a holy day, since to him all days are God's.[4]

While admitting that some Native Americans believed in concepts like reincarnation, Eastman found much harmony between his former beliefs and the teachings of the Bible. In fact, he came to see more common principles between Native beliefs and Jesus than he did between the Christian world and the teachings of Jesus. In contrast to the generosity he saw in his childhood, he became disenchanted with the materialism that seemed to undergird contemporary life and even Christian enterprises. As he began his work with the YMCA, he asked himself how the tribal friends of his youth "were so imbued with the spirit of worship, while much church-going among white and nominally Christian Indians led often to such very small results."[5]

An older man had listened attentively to the Bible study Eastman led among the youth in one Native community. The man attended every meeting for a week. Finally, Eastman called on him to give his views. After a long silence, the man said, "I have come to the conclusion that this Jesus was an Indian. He was opposed to material acquirement and to great possessions. He was inclined to peace. He was as unpractical as any Indian and set no price upon his labor of love. These are not the principles upon which the white man has founded his civilization."[6]

Prophecies and Powwows

Eastman wrote about values and traditions and even prophecies that seemed to point from his childhood faith to the coming of Christianity. He reported evidence of a Sioux prophet foretelling fifty years in advance the coming of the white man.[7] Other tribes told similar stories. The Spokane people, for example, told of a medicine man, Circling Raven, who saw a vision of two men with strange clothes and white skin getting out of a canoe and carrying what looked like a bundle of leaves. Circling Raven believed he heard the Creator of all, Quilent-sat-men, say to him, "Pay attention to the marks on those leaves. They are the Leaves of Life."[8]

Most of the missionaries, though, did not recognize how God had prepared the tribes for their arrival. They were good men, wrote Eastman, but "imbued with the narrowness of their age."[9] The preachers taught that they alone had a real God and what the Natives had formerly thought sacred were "inventions of the devil."[10] They set about not only to teach the Bible but to teach civilization. As one official put it, "Kill the Indian and save the man."[11]

The government-sponsored boarding schools, run from roughly 1875 to 1926, were built not only to educate the Native students but also to cleanse the heathenness from them.[12] As recently as 2008, Canadian Prime Minister Stephen Harper apologized for the negative influence of these schools. He said they "created a void in many lives and communities."[13]

I could catch a glimpse of that void as the service ended in Denver. By now, in the stands, men had donned outfits bristling with feathers and women smoothed out beaded dresses in bright reds, blues, and yellows. I couldn't help but notice the contrast between this extravagant color on the perimeter of the arena and the subdued little group in the center.

After the service ended, I had just a few moments to speak with Richard Silversmith before the public address announcer belted out "Welcome, Denver!" and we had to hustle out of the way. Silversmith told me that even the use of the small drum in their service was controversial. "At a lot of our churches back home," he said, "we can't use the drum."

"Really!" I exclaimed. I didn't realize how resistant Native American churches remained, even to something like a small drum.

The woman who had played guitar was listening in on our conversation. "Yes," she said, "it's forbidden to bring them to church."

I asked about the powwow itself. I wanted to know, had they heard of Christians participating in powwows? And if so, did these believers find it a spiritual experience? "Oh, yeah," said Silversmith. "If you pray and meditate, it's what works for you."

That confirmed what I had already heard, and made me even more curious as I walked across the dirt floor of the arena and found some stairs up to a seat where I could watch the proceedings.

Some months earlier, I had the chance to meet Meredith Winston, a blonde woman married to a Native American. She said the family of her husband, Greg, had become Christians and then had met Jonathan Maracle. He changed their whole way of thinking about their culture and how they could incorporate it into their faith in Christ. Maracle performed Native-style songs and used the drum and feathered regalia. Meredith said often the powwow begins with a prayer in Jesus's name. "When Greg dances," she said, "it's worship to him."

During the summer, the powwow has become almost a weekly event for Meredith's family. They bring a cooler of food, the kids come, people dance, and Greg's brother plays on one of the drumming teams. Although Greg wears a suit to his office job and his parents attend a predominantly white church, the powwow connects them to their cultural roots.

The idea of Christians being involved in a powwow is still controversial and not widely accepted by Native American churches. A Lakota Sioux man, Richard Twiss, in his book *One Church Many Tribes*, told the story of meeting with some Native Christians at a camping area on a reservation. The place where they met was right next to the powwow grounds. But many of the Christian Natives would not walk the several hundred yards over to the powwow to visit friends or to watch the celebration. "They had been taught," wrote Twiss, "that many of their own cultural traditions were of the devil and should be avoided now that they were Christians."[14]

Perhaps given this prevailing view among Christian Native Americans, and in light of their treatment by "Christian" whites, it's not surprising that the vast majority of Native Americans have not embraced the Christian faith. Less than 5 percent of Native Americans call themselves Christians today.[15] Currently Native Americans number about 2 million in the United States and 1.3 million in Canada. Of these, about one-quarter live on reservations. There are still 250 different Native languages and dialects used daily.[16]

About twenty years ago, a handful of Native American believers in Jesus began looking for a better way. They began to look for the ways God was involved in their history, their spiritual history. They wrestled with how they could biblically incorporate their cultural ways into their worship of God. Some began burning sage as part of their prayers. Others met in sweat lodges as a place of worship and intercession. Others used a ceremonial pipe in prayer, incorporated rites of passage for their sons and daughters, or displayed traditional artistic religious motifs. Some held Christ-centered powwows in places like Salem, Oregon; Colorado Springs, Colorado; and Pasadena, California.

The late Richard Twiss, who died in 2013, was one of the leaders of this movement. He said he did not use the term "Christian" anymore. He explained, "Among non-believing Indians the word 'Christianity' has come to mean only the abusive religion of the white man."[17] Instead, Twiss said he and a growing number of evangelical Natives had begun to use "the Jesus Way" to describe their faith.

Twiss admitted there are dangers with this kind of experimentation. For example, a religion called the Native American Church has incorporated the hallucinogenic drug peyote into their liturgy. While arguing against this or occultic and idolatrous influences, Twiss also said, "I do not want fleshly fear to be a primary deterrent to discovering a more Native cultural expression of our Christian faith."[18] He said if their hearts remained humble, and if they proceeded in accountability with wise brothers and sisters, he trusted the Holy Spirit to correct any possible errors.

The Worship Circle

I had a chance to experience one of these new Native expressions of faith just four months before my visit to the powwow. On a rainy day in Winnipeg, Manitoba, I picked my way around puddles on the sidewalk beside a building that had two large Native-style murals on it. I entered and saw before me a brightly colored room. A group of people, mostly Native Americans, were sitting in a circle of chairs beneath a tepee-like skylight. I found an empty chair just as the Thursday morning Worship Circle began. In this building, the Indigenous Family Centre, our meeting was taking place not far from Charles Eastman's boyhood forests.

In the center of the circle, Rebecca, a Native American who looked to be in her early twenties, bent over a small table. She lit a clump of some kind of dried grasses on a large shell that was sitting on a wooden stand. The grasses began to produce a fragrant smoke. She called this a smudge and told people just to let the smudge pass if they didn't want it. "We don't want to force this on anybody."

Lifting the smoking shell, she slowly began to offer it to each person in the group. I was the fourth one to receive it. I did as I'd seen the others do. I waved the smoke toward me and then pulled it over my head. It seemed to me like a symbol of the presence of God. But I wondered, is that what I'm supposed to think?

After Rebecca had visited all fourteen people in the circle, she put the smudge back on the table. The smoke continued to rise up toward the skylight, on which rain was pattering. It really seemed like we were all sitting in a tepee with the smoke of the fire rising up in the middle.

The director of the Indigenous Family Centre, Jeanet Sybenga, stood up from her place in the circle and announced the reading for this day. Jeanet, a slim woman with short hair and glasses, said this being June and a time when students faced exams and transitions into the summer, she had been thinking about risks we face in our lives. She had chosen a reading about taking risks. She passed out a sheet on which she had printed a prayer and the words to Matthew 14:22–33. We read the prayer together, and then several people in the circle took turns reading the story, which told how Jesus and then Peter walked on the water.

After the reading, Jeanet said, "We are sometimes called to step out in faith, not knowing whether we will be able to do it or not." She talked about the feeling of sinking. Even in a storm, "having the faith that the Creator is going to be there. He's going to be the one reaching out a hand to help us up. Or maybe it's someone else the Creator puts in our life."

She then asked the group if anyone would like to comment. One woman said, "If I was Peter, and Jesus said, 'Walk on the water,' I wouldn't have wanted to get out of the boat."

Rick added, "I think what Jeanet said was very good. Faith is a gift. Jesus asks us to walk on the water and we only sink if we have no faith."

After a few more comments, Megan, another young Native woman, went to the table in the center that held the smoking grass and picked up a small, smooth stone. She said, "Feel free to share, and if you don't feel like sharing, you can pass."

Megan started by talking about workshops she's been going to and how her parents have supported her through a difficult time. "I feel like I'm walking on water," she said. "I'm in a rough spot. I'm still bad with alcohol. If I have ever hurt anybody here, any bad words, I'm sorry for that thing. I was in denial."

As Megan spoke, everyone in the group listened quietly. When she finished, she passed the stone to the person on her left.

A middle-aged woman, Joy, told about attending a ceremony for her daughter's graduation from grade seven. "She was happy and I was happy." Joy passed on the stone, and gradually it made its way around to each person. A few handed the rock to the next person without speaking. One man said only, "I'm happy to be here."

When the rock reached Megan again, Rebecca rose to her feet once more. She picked up a small drum and began to sing in a Native language. Her voice was beautiful, and as she sang, she beat the drum slowly in the beginning, then faster in the middle and slowly again at the end.

After a closing prayer by Henk DeBruyn, a soft-spoken man with a gray beard, several members of the group left for the kitchen to prepare lunch. We gathered in the adjacent room, which had tables, chairs, and a Native-style mural along one wall.

As we ate soup and bannock, a kind of bread that was cut into two-inch cubes, I had a chance to learn more about the Worship Circle. James Houle, a thin man with long hair and a wispy beard, told me he had grown up in a residential school run by nuns. They did not allow the burning of sweet grass, but he didn't see a problem with the smudge. He said, "You'll notice in our circle we talk about the Bible, about our Indian ways, our teachings. They coincide. They don't clash."

Houle liked the equality of the circle. He said anyone could come, whether children, men, or women. "You can have a big businessman here who owns five companies, and you might have a drunk that lives in his back lane," Houle remarked. In the circle, they are both treated the same. Houle appreciated that, and he liked how everyone could see each other's face. In churches, he said, only one person talks and everyone faces the same direction. "All you see is the back of this person's head."

As Houle left, he introduced me to Sarah, a young woman dressed nicely in business attire. Sarah told me she's from the Ojibwe tribe and she's been studying theology and culture at an organization in town. "A lot of our Native people don't know their culture," she said. They don't speak the language, they don't know the songs or dances, and they don't know the customs. "We're starting to learn it again." She laughed as she added, "We are adopting this and this and this from different tribes and getting our people totally mixed up."

She said she's on this journey of discovery mainly because of what God did in her life. "For many years I didn't like being Native," Sarah admitted. "I didn't like the culture. I didn't like Native men. To be brown was a taboo. I was born wrong. The white people were the ones who were right." She wrestled with her identity and asked, "Was God wrong that He created the red people? Was it a mistake?"

After a lot of prayer, Sarah said her perspective began to change little by little. "God revealed to me there was good and bad in every tribe." She learned to appreciate her cultural heritage, while also recognizing the presence of negative aspects, like black magic.

She said in churches on the reservation where she grew up, they still couldn't use feathers or drums or chants or sweet grass. If you do, she said, "They are just going to up and walk out."

Now Sarah relishes what she has been learning. "It's like fresh ground for us again. We have to find it again. It's just a reopening thing."

After lunch, as some of the Natives remained to work on a moccasin-making craft, Jeanet told me many of the Natives feel the same way Sarah does. "People really want to learn about who they are," she said. "It's so much of an identity thing. Where do I come from? What is the spirituality of our people?" She said she'd talked to Natives who tried European-style church, "but when they go to an aboriginal ceremony, they say it's like coming home. There's something that connects at the heart level."

But does that kind of spirituality belong in a Christian center? That's a question Henk DeBruyn, the founder of the Indigenous Family Centre, faced when he arrived in Winnipeg in 1974. As a pastor who had formerly served in the inner city of Detroit, DeBruyn told me he brought with him a conviction that every aspect of life can be redeemed, including culture. The big question for him was, "How does redemption work?"

In the beginning, he preached and even picked up Natives to come to the Sunday services. For his own education, he read first-hand accounts by Natives about their spirituality. He studied the mythological stories. Often he could not figure out the stories. He said, "I just let it sit."

On the one hand, DeBruyn met Native American Christian leaders who would have nothing to do with the pipe or the drum. On the other, he encountered statements like, "It's fine to pray to God, but when I pray to my grandfather it has more effect."

Eventually, as the Centre grew, DeBruyn said he grew as well. He became less materialistic and he released control. "They themselves set the boundaries," he said. "They knew what was right from what was wrong, what is healing, what is not healing, what is of God, and what is not of God."

He remembered when they first planned the Worship Circle. Some of the women talked about how the burning sweet grass provided a sense of being cleansed. Others said we are cleansed by the blood of Christ; we don't need the smudge. DeBruyn suggested they try it and see how it worked.

"At this point I would miss the smudge," DeBruyn said. "There is a quieting thing about it." He said one of the murals on the wall of the main room depicts the burning grass. It shows a rainbow-colored column rising up to the sun from the hands of a central figure. The column of smoke represents prayer, explained DeBruyn. It rises up from the people in the picture. From the sun, seven drops fall down. That represents the tears of God. "God crying with us," stated DeBruyn. "God walks with us even in our tough times."

DeBruyn also explained the use of the rock. Native languages, he said, distinguish between the animate and the inanimate. Stones are considered animate. During the Worship Circle they will often explain that the rock, as one of the oldest elements of creation, is like a grandfather. The stone will hear their stories and hold them.

Walking on Water

As DeBruyn incorporated new concepts into the Indigenous Family Centre, he was held accountable by oversight committees of his denomination, the Christian Reformed Church. One time, a supervisory group came for a visit. One man heard one of DeBruyn's staff use the term "Creator" instead of "God." The visitor asked,

"Which Creator?" The staff person replied, "Are there more?" De-Bruyn listened to this and thought, "If you talk about the Creator, you talk about the Creator. There's only one Creator. He doesn't have competition."

DeBruyn told me that many times along the way he thought of the story of walking on the water. He felt that he had stepped outside of the boat he had been taught to use. "This is not the way we were supposed to do things. It would be a lot safer if we would preach from the front and sing some hymns. Then everybody knows that everything is okay."

He said he found himself motivated more by the people and their need than by whether or not a particular method would work. "I've always said, Christ loves people more than I do, and He continues to reveal Himself in ways that people recognize."

Now, many of DeBruyn's early critics have adopted some of the practices pioneered by the Indigenous Family Centre. Even some of the Native American Christian leaders in the city now incorporate the pipe or the drum in prayer and worship.

DeBruyn said many times when people wanted solid answers from him, he didn't have them. "I was walking on water, and if you asked Peter, 'How can you walk on water?' he wouldn't know."

At the Western Event Center in Denver, the drums had begun in earnest. In one of the groups, eight men sat in a circle around their drum and pounded out a throbbing beat as two women, clothed in beautiful jingling dresses, swirled around the arena. With lifted arms, tracing the arc of their movements, they skipped and twirled. After they finished their dance, two men, called fancy dancers, followed. These men wore elaborate regalia, with feathers on their heads, hips, and shoulders. From their arms and wrists hung long fringes that they could twirl as they danced. They spun these with both arms as their legs pounded the ground ferociously. Sometimes with one foot pointed on the ground as a pivot, they would use their other leg to spin. Other times, they would crouch down, touch the dirt with both hands, and lunge forward. As they did, the drummers sang a piercing, haunting song.

I found the sights and sounds thrilling. I envied those dancers. If they wanted to dance with God in mind, they could express themselves in ways I had never been able to do.

As I left through the big doors, I realized that Meredith Winston had been right. The powwow did open with prayer. The man who prayed said, "We have the promise of a Savior, our almighty Creator." I didn't know all of what this man believed, and I certainly didn't know what motivated the dancers in front of me. But the man who prayed concluded as Meredith said he would: "I thank you that we are a people that will call upon you in times like this and thank you for your blessings. I pray all of this in the name of Jesus."

I drove home wondering what a powwow worship service would be like. What if dance was the main thing people gathered to do when they came together for worship? What if there was no sermon? What if the large group broke up into little Bible discussion circles? What if they passed a rock as a way to give everyone a chance to speak? What if the gathering took place outdoors as often as possible? Could some of these formats help people who don't come from a Native American background?

After all my travels, I could see many possibilities for the worship of Christ and the service of God. So many more than I ever imagined. But how to see that multicolored world unfold? How to get from here to there?

Part Two

BOUNDARY
BREAKERS

7

Boundary Breakers

My head was spinning. I had recently made two trips to Asia. Now, before a third Asian journey, I was squeezing in a vacation. It was 2007, and my thirteen-year-old son and I were blasting our way past semitrailer trucks, trying to hit Iowa by dinnertime. My son had disappeared in the backseat of our minivan, wrapped in a blanket, absorbed in a video game. I had time to think. I watched as the high plains made way for fields of corn. Overhead, a vast prairie sky dotted with clouds stretched out to the horizon.

Very different scenes were tumbling through my brain. I thought of the people I'd seen and places I'd been. I remembered an odd procession of women who passed me on a narrow street in India. There were about seven of them, wearing neon-bright saris of orange, pink, or green. The gray-haired woman in front pounded on two drums that hung around her neck. I paused at the doorway to an ashram as they walked by me. Then I entered the building. Inside the tall stone structure I met a bearded man dressed in an orange robe. He told me that he followed Jesus as a Hindu *sannyasi*, one who has renounced worldly pursuits. That's the reason he wore the saffron color. He explained how he had dedicated himself to a celibate life of seeking God and mentoring others.

I thought of the gold, red, and green carved dragon that twisted and turned along the steps that led up to a temple in Thailand and remembered my conversations with the ex-monk, then clad in a T-shirt and jeans, walking up the steps in front of me. There were so many fascinating people. A handsome young African man came to mind. Dressed in a long golden shirt, he stopped to chat with me at a Thailand conference. He told me about his Muslim childhood in an East African village.

I realized there was something similar between these people. For one thing, many of them avoided the term "Christian." In one way or another, these believers called themselves Muslims, Hindus, Buddhists, or Native Americans who followed Jesus.

They didn't emphasize the labels, though, and that's what really got me thinking as I drove past rolls of hay sitting on fields of stubble. The labels were just words on the surface. Deeper down, they held beliefs about the Bible and what it tells us to do and doesn't tell us to do. I realized I had heard people saying similar things about the Bible but in different ways. I also had observed some common characteristics in the behavior of the people I had met.

What are those biblical foundations, I wondered? More than that, if those principles come from the Bible, then what might these insights mean for anyone, from any culture? How can these movements provide hope even to people like Craig in Colorado or my own son now dozing in the backseat?

Night was falling when we finally arrived at our hotel in Iowa. Staggering out of the van and dropping our luggage in our room, we headed straight for the indoor pool. My son came to life as he leaped into the water. He swam under my legs and raced me from one side of the tiny pool to the other. Later, after showers, my son climbed into bed. I turned off the light but didn't go to sleep myself. I stood by the sink in the bathroom.

I lingered there, because everything was coming together in my head. I realized several streams ran underneath all the geography I'd covered. I jotted down a list of biblical ideas that I had heard everywhere I traveled. As I stared at what I'd written in the dim light, I realized there were four main principles.

In the years that followed, I have basically left that list intact. My later travels only confirmed what I perceived there in that Iowa hotel room.

I have thought a lot more about the implications of these principles. Each of them has the power to break down walls that keep people separated from Jesus. Each of them can help believers in Jesus get beyond their places of stagnation. Taken together, they can demolish unnecessary barriers that believers in Jesus have built up around God, barriers that aren't biblical at all.

I began to think of these four principles as boundary breakers. In this section, I'll explain these principles and illustrate each of them with stories from my travels.

The first principle is as old as faith in Jesus itself.

8

Put the Book in Its Place

Cal warned me. As I corresponded with him about my upcoming trip to Bangladesh, he told me that some people who visit a Christ-centered jamaat find themselves going away a little disappointed. They expect to find something exotic, Cal explained, and what they see instead looks a lot like a small-group Bible study.

It turned out Cal was right. Whether it was in a crowded kitchen in Bangladesh or under a tepee-like skylight in Winnipeg or in a small apartment in India, in my travels I almost always ended up watching people gather around the Bible. Far from being disappointed, though, I kept thinking there was something profound about these little clusters of people seated around the holy book. The Bible seemed to have a central role not only in the lives of believers but also in the lives of nonbelievers.

Jay, the man I met in India, told me about a time when a satsang met in a home in a poor part of his city. Soon after the participants took their places on the floor, a faint, unpleasant odor came into the room. At this point, no one in the group other than the leader had decided to follow Yeshu. They all considered themselves Hindus. They were discussing the story of Jesus watching the widow put two coins into the treasury. The satsang leader asked, "Why would Jesus say she gave more than the rich people?"

The group discussed the widow's generosity. Then they began to talk about the many widows in their own city, many of whom were destitute. One person said, "Yeah, if I saw a widow in need, I would help her."

As the satsang continued, the odor in the room began to get worse. Eventually someone commented on it. They realized the stench came from under the doorway at the front of the house. One of the people got up and opened the door. There on the cement in front of them lay an old woman. She wore the white sari of a widow. She had a gash on her forehead and she had soiled her clothes. A cloud of flies buzzed around her in the black night.

One person in the group yelled at her, "What are you doing here? Get out of here!" The others argued about what to do.

Then a woman spoke up. "Wait! This is Sadguru Yeshu testing us. We heard the story of the widow. He was speaking to us in the satsang, telling us we need to help someone." The whole group agreed. The women gathered the widow in, cleaned her wound, fed her, bathed her, and put clean clothes on her. The next day, Jay helped several group members bring the woman to a facility run by Mother Teresa's organization. A week later, the widow died.

"That woman died with dignity," Jay told me, "and the fellowship started to understand what it means to be the satsang of the Lord."

The participants in this satsang, like many of the people I met on my travels, had been changed by the power of the Bible. When they met together to discuss it, they encountered a transforming influence. This happened even with people who had not yet decided to follow Jesus.

Rick Brown, an expert in Bible translation, met with me at a conference in Thailand and told me how he has seen this power firsthand. He said believers in Jesus don't need to defend the Bible or attack the Qur'an with Muslims. We just encourage Muslim friends to read all the holy books, as the Qur'an itself instructs them to do.

As Rick explained this to me, he used a hand gesture I'd seen other experts use. In the beginning, he said, the Muslim's view of the Qur'an might be far higher than the Bible. In particular, they might view current translations of the Bible as corrupted and untrustworthy. As he spoke, he lifted up one hand, representing their view of the Qur'an, and kept his other hand on the table. But then, he said, as the person reads the Bible, almost without exception, it rises in their estimation. Gradually he brought his hands level in front of him. Eventually, while the Muslim still shows respect for the Qur'an, he said, the Bible often becomes the book he or she wants to read. He lifted his Bible hand above his head.

A Different Picture

As I traveled back and forth between Asia and North America, I began to reflect on the contrasts I was seeing. I also became aware of an intriguing parallel. The contrast was that as I thought of the central picture of faith in Christ in the West, I didn't picture a small group gathered in a circle around a Bible. I pictured crowds of parishioners sitting in rows listening to a preacher. Of course the preacher would almost always teach from the Bible. And of course many churches would contain small groups that might study the Bible in homes. So the Bible was certainly in the picture. It just wasn't as centrally in the picture as it was with the groups I visited overseas. The Western picture I had in my mind was more of a pastor-centered than Bible-centered gathering.

Some research studies suggest that my mental picture reflects reality. The Bible is increasingly sliding toward the periphery of the Christian life. Of every five Protestant churchgoers in the United

States, only one reads his or her Bible every day.[1] According to a Gallup poll in 2000, slightly more than half of Americans (59 percent) still read the Bible at least occasionally, but that number has declined from 73 percent in the 1980s.[2] In Europe the statistics have become much worse. In Italy only one in four had read any passage from the Bible in the year prior to a 2008 survey.[3]

This declining Bible use has led to dwindling knowledge about the contents of the Bible. Only half of all Christians in the United States can name all four Gospels. Four of every ten Christians in this country think that "Do unto others as you would have them do unto you" is one of the Ten Commandments.[4]

At Wheaton College, a leading evangelical school, a professor surveyed incoming freshmen and found the same kind of ignorance about basic biblical teaching. One-third of the students could not put the following in chronological order: Abraham, the Old Testament prophets, the death of Christ, and Pentecost.[5]

One of my friends teaches at a Christian college in Florida. He said not only do many incoming students not know their Bible, but many of them don't even take a Bible to school. They don't read it, and they don't seem to like to read in general. One professor gets around this problem by giving freshmen an audio Bible file.

One problem with not reading the Bible and relying on pastors and spiritual experts for advice is that believers in Jesus can begin to live within the confines of what makes a good sermon or a good book. The Bible doesn't always fit within these boundaries. The Bible gets under a person's skin.

I have a friend who grew up in a Hindu family in Delhi, India. As a teenager, he decided he would like to grow spiritually. He began reading both the Bhagavad Gita and the Bible. At first, he didn't like the Bible at all. But then he noticed a strange thing happening: "The Bible began to read me."

I think everyone who has read the Bible with an openness to its teaching knows the uncomfortable and liberating feeling my friend described.

Apparently the Bible also still contains some fascination for young people who don't attend church. A remarkable LifeWay Research study in 2009 found that unchurched young people have more interest in joining a group Bible study than most Christians realize. When asked to respond to the statement "I would be willing to study the Bible if a friend asked me to," 61 percent of unchurched twentysomethings said yes. They responded yes at a rate 20 percent higher than older people did. Similarly, when asked if they would be willing to join a small group to study the Bible, 46 percent of the young people said yes. This rate of affirmative responses was again 27 percent higher than the rate for older generations.[6]

These young adults seem to crave something that Christians themselves have gotten away from. They want what the people I visited overseas seem to have.

For a Christianized world in which Bible use is on the decline, I think the first lesson from the radical approaches used at the places I visited is to return to an old truth. Bring the Bible back into the center of group gatherings. Discuss the actual writings of the Bible. Invite unchurched friends to join in.

The New Orality

This brings me to the intriguing parallel I began to notice as I traveled. In Asia, many of the people I saw interacting with the Bible weren't reading it. They were telling stories from it.

In India I remember watching Arun's eyes light up as he spoke with enthusiasm to the young men sitting on the floor around him. Although Arun sat in front of a Bible placed on a stand, he looked directly at each person in the circle as he told the story of Peter walking on the water. He wasn't reading the story. He was telling it from memory. He and the other members of his team in this city purposely use the Bible in this way.

They tell the story orally, explained one of Arun's team members, because "that is the traditional way to disseminate spiritual truths here in Asia." They tell the story with an open Bible in front of them to emphasize that the spoken story is anchored in the Bible's written account. When the home satsang encountered the widow at their doorway, they were using this same approach.

Across the world, this way of approaching the Bible as spoken stories has become a rapidly growing trend. Almost every large mission agency now runs some kind of program devoted to orality. According to an estimate from one mission research group, 70 percent of the world now prefers to learn orally.[7] Some of these oral learners are illiterate or semiliterate. But many, like the Indian university students I joined in the satsang, would simply rather learn through stories told out loud.

The fascinating thing I discovered as I traveled is that this preference for oral learning increasingly describes the literate West as well. The technology revolution has created new generations of people who learn primarily through audio-visual means. Our world has increasingly become a postliterate world.

Marshall McLuhan, writing back in the early 1960s, saw this trend advancing. He wrote, "Electric technology seems to favor the inclusive and participational spoken word over the specialist written word."[8] This tech-savvy preference for the spoken word has been called "secondary orality." According to one mission researcher, "This secondary orality, now endemic in our world today, is causing us to think, process information, make decisions, and socially organize ourselves more and more like oral peoples rather than literate ones."[9]

Surveys of literate nations, like the United States, hint at the trend McLuhan identified. According to a 2003 National Assessment of Adult Literacy survey, only 13 percent of Americans demonstrate proficient literacy. The literacy level for more than four in ten Americans reaches only basic or below-basic levels.[10] In Canada and Europe surveys have found similar results.[11]

I wonder, as I so often did when I traveled, is what's happening out there providing an answer to us who live over here? Faced with rising levels of functional illiteracy, a growing number of Christian leaders now scramble to figure out how to reach oral learners. This process began many years ago. In the 1970s Trevor McIlwain of New Tribes Mission tried to find a new way to communicate biblical truth to a tribal community in the Philippines that could not read or write. He decided to start at the beginning of the Bible and teach his way through to the end using spoken stories from the Bible. He called this method Chronological Bible Teaching. McIlwain discovered that this method helped the tribal people grasp God's character and the Christian faith.

His success caught the attention of two Southern Baptist missionaries, who adapted McIlwain's storytelling approach. They called this method "storying."[12]

In some ways, McIlwain and the others were rediscovering a primary means of communication used within the Bible itself. Much of the content of the Bible began as stories passed on from person to person. Followers of Yahweh retold the story of Abraham for five hundred years before it was finally included in a written account called Genesis. Jesus used stories so often that his disciples asked him about it. "Why do you speak to the people in parables?" they asked.[13] According to Mark, Jesus almost always used this form of communication.[14]

Now several ministries and organizations exist to teach people how to use Bible stories in this way. They have names like OneStory, Simply the Story, International Orality Network, and Story4All.

Novelli's Teens

As these ministries have proliferated, some have caught the attention of youth workers in Western nations, workers who often struggle to figure out how to inspire teens who no longer respond to traditional literate approaches.

One of those youth workers, Michael Novelli, went to a storying workshop in the United States put on by a mission agency. At first, Novelli wondered why he was there. He had been searching for a way to help the teens in his youth group in Chicago connect with the Bible and had used inductive studies, chapter analysis, *lectio divina*, thematic approaches, and many other methods. But only a handful of students in Novelli's group showed any interest in what they were reading, no matter what Novelli tried.

Worse, Novelli guessed that he and the other youth group leaders were actually preventing kids from asking deeper questions. "It felt as though we were digesting the Bible for our students and regurgitating it back to them in bite-size pieces, like birds to their young," Novelli recalled.

The new approach Novelli learned was something he had never heard of before. The workshop leader, a missionary to Africa named John Witte, told more than thirty Bible stories, mostly from memory. He led the group in dialogue about each story. Novelli knew all of these stories very well, having heard them dozens of times. He had even studied some of them in college. But as the workshop participants dug into these well-known plots, Novelli couldn't believe how much they were getting out of them. "I was amazed at how captivated we all were by these stories," he said.

Novelli went home from the workshop determined to try yet another new approach with his students, the storying method. During the summer, he picked a set of stories that would span the whole Bible and would take his youth group nine months to cover. He thought about creative ways the young people would tell, retell, and discuss these stories.

At first, the kids in Novelli's group didn't respond the way he hoped they would. He plied the group with questions about the first story, but the students just offered puzzled responses: "What does this have to do with everyday life?" or, "So when are you going to teach us?"

Novelli knew the kids thought he was crazy. "I felt like we were going through a detox program together," he said. Novelli assured the students that they were growing into adults and as they looked into these stories, God would show each of them meaningful truths. God would use them to teach each other.

As the weeks went on and as the kids studied creation, the fall of Adam and Eve, and Cain and Abel, they began to remark on connections they were seeing between the stories. They would offer observations without being asked.

One week, a girl from the group brought a friend who had expressed interest in the stories. This girl, who had never heard these biblical accounts before, said, "Tonight I realized that the stories you're telling are going in a different direction than my own life." A boy who attended the group felt inspired by the discussion about God's covenant with Abraham. He realized part of that covenant was to act as a blessing to others. He initiated opportunities for the group to serve the homeless and reach out to students at his school.

By the end of the school year, Novelli threw a party for the students and their parents. At the cookout he gave an opportunity for the kids to tell their parents what they had learned. One of them said, "I couldn't stop thinking about the stories. Some of the questions were so difficult that they made me want to go and search for the answers."

Novelli was hooked. He began teaching other youth group leaders about storying. He wrote a book called *Shaped by the Story*. He concluded, "Storying is unpredictable, unsettling, and full of wonder and moments of awakening."[15]

Other youth group leaders report similar results. They find that stories connect with youth culture. According to Tommy Jones, author of *Postmodern Youth Ministry*, "Narrative is becoming the primary means of telling beliefs."[16]

A friend of mine, Bryan Thompson, learned about storying when working with nomadic people in North Africa. When asked to preach at a church in Ireland, he turned the whole morning sermon into a storying session.

He first told his audience the account of Elisha and the widow in 2 Kings 4. As the people listened, he told the story from memory, not word for word, but true in all the details. Then he asked members of the congregation to pair up and tell the story to each other as best they could remember it. After that he asked simple questions about the plot, such as, "What was the widow supposed to do to the door?" People shouted out the answers from where they sat.

Then he moved to analysis questions. For example, "In going to Elisha, what was the widow deciding to do?"

Finally, he asked for application. He asked questions like, "Do any of you know someone who has been in a desperate situation and God has led them to take some difficult path?" One man told of a time when he needed an operation but couldn't pay for it because he was out of work. He recounted the surprising ways people contributed to his need. After he paid for the operation, he got a job and the mysterious donations stopped. "I just believe God provides," the man said.

At the end, Thompson simply let the comments of the audience speak for themselves. He closed in prayer and then said, "Share the story with those who haven't heard it. You know it."[17]

Storying in Chiang Mai

One Friday in Chiang Mai, Thailand, I unexpectedly got to witness storying for myself. I was leading a weeklong meeting, and on Friday afternoon we finally had a break in our schedule. Twelve of us decided to use our free time to visit Ben Jones, a man who works in a part of Chiang Mai near an old temple. More than three hundred thousand people live in this area, and almost all of them are Buddhists.

Jones, a tall man from the Pacific Islands, had learned the Thai language well. Several times a week he made trips into the neighborhoods of this area. He had a simple goal: find people who would like to hear a story about God. Once he found a family who wanted to listen, he would get to know them a little bit and then would tell them a Bible story. Afterward, he would ask if they wanted him to come back in a week to tell another story.

After only three weeks of doing this, Jones already had eight different families he was visiting each week to tell stories. By the time he told two or three stories, he would encourage his listeners to tell the stories to their friends or family.

I joined our little group as we followed Jones along the hot pavement, up one little street and down another. We passed the old temple. Barking dogs ran up to us as we walked by the gates of nicer homes. We meandered past metal-roofed homes with painted cement walls and concrete courtyards ringed with ivy.

Then we stopped at the dwelling of a man who owned a couple of shiny red *songthaews*, truck taxis, which were parked in their metal-roofed courtyard. The man and the woman of the house, along with their daughter, listened to the story Jones told. Then the woman pointed to her face. She said she had heard that Jesus could heal. She wanted us to pray for a nervous twitch she had. Jones prayed, and we all silently joined him. She also agreed to have Jones come back the next week, at 6 p.m. on Wednesday, to tell another story. Then we rode back to our hotel in one of the family's taxis.

As I watched the wife and her husband wave at us as they backed the songthaew into the swirl of Thailand traffic, they seemed grateful for our visit and our prayers. I wondered if they would welcome Jones back again. If so, what effect might these stories have?

Watching Jones tell his stories made me imagine Jesus telling stories to the crowds that followed him. In his afterword to *The*

Message, Eugene Peterson remarked on the stories of Jesus. "More often than not, one or another of them lodges unnoticed in our consciousness," Peterson wrote, "and then, unexpectedly, begins to release insights, to create new perspectives, to shift the very ground beneath us so that we find ourselves reeling, reaching out for wisdom."[18]

I wonder if maybe in the narrative-oriented, secondary orality world we live in, it would be good to add another kind of Bible memorization to our spiritual disciplines. Maybe we could memorize whole stories, not so much the exact wording but the plot and the key details. I think that could help us dialogue with a world that increasingly values story and increasingly learns through the spoken word.

If you would like to get a taste of storying, I invite you and your group to try the Boundless Jesus Bible Study at the end of this book. This ten-week Bible study will give you a chance to grapple with the stories of Jesus using the storying method. The experience will also allow you to see, hear, and practice some of the approaches I'll recommend in the next chapters.

So the first boundary breaker principle simply involves the Bible: Move the Bible back into the center of group gatherings and discuss it together. Reclaim the Bible in a way that brings fresh relevance to an electronic, increasingly oral generation.

9

Move Toward Jesus

As I traveled through Asia, and as I watched people gather around the Bible, I perceived a deliberate blurring of lines. The groups I visited contained both Jesus-followers and other people who were simply curious. In India, most satsang participants still called themselves Hindus. What did each of them believe? Who was inside the group and who was outside? It wasn't clear.

Later, after reflecting on what I'd seen, I realized I had encountered a fundamental principle of these movements. Labels don't define them. Organizational allegiance doesn't identify them. As a group they seek to become closer to Jesus, and this is what sets them apart. They emphasize a process of growth that often begins before the seeker makes any commitment to Christ. They entrust their progress to the work of the Holy Spirit in their midst.

I began to believe the principle behind this growth process, a principle that has several facets and has the potential to break down walls between the gospel and people who consider themselves outsiders. It also has the potential to help every believer make real progress in demonstrating the actions and attitudes taught in the Bible.

I heard one of the best illustrations of this principle in a hotel room in Thailand. I had come back to the same Thailand complex where I met Randy at the very beginning of my journey. Now I was serving at a conference that brought together believers in Jesus who work in the Muslim world. The conference organizers claimed the three hundred people who attended comprised the largest gathering of Muslim-world church planters in history. My job was to interview some of these workers.

One day, Carl, a man who lives in rural Africa, agreed to talk with me. The conference organizers provided us a quiet hotel room, we wedged a couple of chairs between the bed and the wall, and Carl told me his story.

For more than fifteen years, Carl has made his home among Muslim subsistence farmers. He and his team give their neighbors agricultural advice. They also encourage their friends to meet together to talk about stories from the Bible.

A village woman who helps with an agriculture project told Carl, "I would like my husband to hear the Word of God." Carl agreed, but added, "I want you to go home and ask your relatives what they think of having a small group that would meet to study the Word of God. Let me know if people find that agreeable."

The woman soon came to Carl and reported, "Yes, people would like that."

In this part of Africa, Carl told me, usually Muslims do not understand the Arabic words of the Qur'an. They have to rely on their imams to interpret the words for them. "There's a deep sense that they don't know the Word of God very well."

When Carl met with the woman and her husband, he came into their home and sat down with the little group of relatives gathered there. He began by telling a Bible story from Genesis that would be familiar to the group because the story also appears in the Qur'an. Then he simply let the group discuss the implications.

After only a couple of meetings, Carl noticed that the woman's husband picked up the points of the stories quickly. This man also helped draw out other members of the group. After a silent pause, this man might comment, "Okay, well, no one spoke on the ladies' side."

Carl decided the husband was already able to take over for him. Carl took the man aside privately and asked, "What do you think of you and your wife leading the meeting?" Carl explained he would meet with this couple once a week to talk about Scripture. For the group meeting itself, though, Carl trusted that the Holy Spirit could help this man and his wife facilitate. The man said, "Yeah, I'll do that."

The fact that a Muslim farmer, who hadn't even encountered the stories about Jesus yet, would lead discussions about the accounts of Abraham, Jacob, or Samuel, suggests a different way of viewing the body of Christ. Where does this farmer fit within the fellowship of Jesus-followers? Is he in or is he out?

The Centered Set

In 1994 mission professor Paul Hiebert suggested two ways of looking at the question of who is in and who is out.[1] Hiebert explained the difference between bounded sets and centered sets. A bounded set defines people by whether they fit inside or outside of a boundary. A centered set defines them by how close they come to a middle point.

Australian ranches provide a good illustration of these two models.[2] If the livestock graze near settled communities, the ranchers build fences to keep their animals from wandering off. That's a bounded set. On the other hand, if the ranchers live in the outback, far from human habitation, they might dig wells instead. The cows might roam away from the well temporarily, but they continue to return to the water. That's a centered set.

Institutional Christianity has emphasized the bounded set. The Bible contains teaching that can reflect both a bounded-set and centered-set perspective, but it's the bounded-set point of view that seems to win out in Christian practice.[3] If a person believes the core precepts of the faith, they are in. If they don't, they are out. Christian language has reflected this view. "Heathen." "Saved." Out, in.

People like Carl emphasize the centered set instead. Muslim family leaders like the farmer can decide what they want to call themselves. They can begin obeying the Bible right away. They can even provide spiritual leadership to others, with a little assistance.

Increasingly, this centered-set thinking has begun to change the way people in the Christianized world behave as well. Jim Tebbe, for seven years the head of InterVarsity's mission program and director of the massive Urbana mission conference, told me about a change that has occurred lately within InterVarsity's campus ministry. Tebbe said when he joined InterVarsity as a college student, the members of his campus group would lead evangelistic Bible studies and share their faith until people gave their lives to Christ. At that point they would ask the new believers if they wanted to join the InterVarsity group. Now, Tebbe said, InterVarsity's research has shown that a third of the people who are actively a part of the InterVarsity chapters call themselves nonbelievers. "That absolutely clobbered me," Tebbe said. "They are looking for community first. They are attracted to Jesus, and they are moving in that direction."

With this fact in mind, in 2009 the Urbana leaders decided to provide, right in the midst of their mission conference, an invitation to receive Christ. More than four hundred young people responded. "All of us were weeping," Tebbe recalled. Many participants came to that conference investigating service opportunities without yet having made a firm commitment to Christ.

These InterVarsity groups, like the African Bible-story gatherings, offer a centered-set inclusiveness. Come investigate, come join us, and we will welcome you wherever you are on the faith journey.

Another study, this one from a large church, showed that this kind of centered-set movement toward Jesus describes the way people actually grow. It's not only a way for seekers to enter into spiritual community, but it's also the way members of those communities demonstrate spiritual growth.

In 2004, Willow Creek Community Church in Chicago, which attracts twenty-three thousand attendees each week, decided to ask some uncomfortable questions about what was actually happening in the spiritual lives of the people in their church. Up to this point, they had gathered basic information on their flock, such as marital status and spiritual background, but now they asked a research firm to help them understand what kind of spiritual development was happening under the surface.

They expected that as church involvement increased, such as attendance at services and participation in volunteer work, they would find that spiritual growth would increase as well. But that's not what they found. Their report, called the REVEAL study, found that those who were the most active in church did not display the highest levels of spiritual attitudes, such as love for God, or spiritual behaviors, such as evangelism and tithing.[4]

The researchers struggled to make sense of the data. If increasing levels of church activity didn't yield equally increasing amounts of spiritual growth, could they find some other factor that would produce the fruit the Bible calls for? They ended up developing a different scale. They asked the congregation to choose a category that best described their relationship with Christ. They offered four options:

- Exploring Christ: "I believe in God, but I am not sure about Christ. My faith is not a significant part of my life."
- Growing in Christ: "I believe in Jesus and I am working on what it means to get to know Him."
- Close to Christ: "I feel really close to Christ and depend on Him daily for guidance."

- Christ-Centered: "My relationship with Jesus is the most important relationship in my life. It guides everything I do."[5]

The Willow Creek researchers found that when they looked at the data this way, "Attitudes and behaviors associated with spiritual growth increased in lockstep with movement along the continuum."[6] Why would measuring a person's sense of their closeness to Christ produce such a strong indicator of their level of spiritual growth? The researchers concluded, "This demonstrates a spiritual heart shift from a self-centered identity to an identity defined by a relationship with Christ."[7] In other words, the Willow Creek researchers created a picture of the church body as a centered set, with Jesus in the middle. As attendees moved into a closer personal posture toward Christ, they displayed higher levels of spiritual attitudes and behaviors.

A centered-set perspective can help faith in Christ go both deeper and wider. For the African Bible groups and the InterVarsity campus chapters, the centered-set perspective helps them throw the doors wide open to a variety of seekers. People who want to investigate faith in Christ don't have to change any labels. They can just come. Willow Creek also finds the centered-set model a way to help a faith community go deeper. As they move closer to Christ, they display deeper levels of spiritual attitudes and actions. Greg Hawkins, the leader of the REVEAL study, said "We truly believe that God revealed new insights to us about the people of our church—and how our church can help them grow closer to Christ."[8]

Kingdom Circles

In both cases, this model seems to fit within a concept Jesus Himself constantly talked about.

In the Middle East in 1981, a frustrated Navigator missionary discovered another word that could describe Willow Creek's centered-set continuum. George and his wife had arrived in the Middle East to teach English at an Arab boys' school. They had left their campus back in the United States where they had a fruitful ministry, using five different methods of evangelism. Now they longed to share their faith with Muslim friends using these approaches. The problem was, nothing worked.

At one point, George and his wife admitted to each other that they were struggling with Arabic and had lost hope. George confessed to his wife, "If we can't figure out how to communicate truth with our Muslim friends, I think we will need to go back to the United States."

Then George read a book that changed his whole perspective. It was called *The Unshakeable Kingdom and the Unchanging Person* by E. Stanley Jones. In the book Jones, who worked in India, explains how much Jesus talks about the kingdom and how little Christians talk about it.

In a magazine article in 1970, Jones wondered why this concept of the kingdom played such a small part in the major creeds of the church. Jones noted that the Apostles' Creed and the Athanasian Creed don't mention the kingdom at all, and the Nicene Creed mentions it only in relation to heaven. "The three great historic creeds summing up Christian doctrine mention once what Jesus mentioned a hundred times," Jones fumed. "Something had dropped out. . . . A vital, vital thing had dropped out. . . . A crippled Christianity went across Europe, leaving a crippled result. . . . A vacuum was left in the soul of Western civilization."[9]

When George read about the kingdom, he thought, "That's it! That's exactly where we need to go." He and his wife did an indepth study of the kingdom of God throughout the Bible. George developed a method of talking to Muslim friends using the concept of the kingdom as the foundation for conversations. After sixteen years in the Middle East, George now teaches about the kingdom in seminars around the world.

George's kingdom language fits the centered-set, Christ-centered continuum. He defines the kingdom as "the reign or rule of God." George said a modern equivalent of the word that Jesus used might be "revolution." "Jesus was talking about real revolution," George asserted.

In the Arab world, George found that he could talk about the kingdom with his Muslim friends in a disarming way, in a way that provided helpful common language for future discussions. He found that discussions about the kingdom could lead to questions about the king. He developed a way of talking about the kingdom using circles.

I met George at the same Thailand event where I met Carl. Over dinner, George sketched out for me these kingdom circles. At his invitation, I also attended one of his seminars in Phoenix, where I began to understand the kingdom circles better.

George might begin a conversation with a Muslim friend by saying, "Do you know what the main teaching was of Isa al-Masih?"

The friend might say, "Was it Christianity?"

George would say, "No, the Messiah never used the word 'Christian.' His main teaching was about the kingdom of God."

George would draw a big circle and say, "Allah has created an eternal kingdom." He would explain that this includes all of God's creation in the universe, and God rules supremely over it. He might use verses like Psalm 145:10–13 or Hebrews 12:28 to describe God's kingdom. Then he would say, "God has a special realm for man in His kingdom, but," and he would point outside the circle, "man has left it." He would then explain that God still offers to man this realm of His kingdom, but He says we must seek His kingdom.

At this point George might ask some questions of his friend. "What are the parts of any kingdom? What might those parts look like in God's kingdom?"

He would talk about traditions and explain how following traditions is not enough to enter the kingdom. He might give a warning from Jesus about this, from Mark 7:1–13. Also he might read Mark

12:29–30 and discuss how easy it is to keep a creed but forget the command to love God.

Then George would draw a smaller circle, with part of the small circle inside the big circle and part outside. He would call this circle Christianity. He would explain that some of the people who call themselves Christians don't try to live according to the kingdom, and some do. He might ask his friend to draw a circle representing Islam. Many times, the friend would also draw a small circle only partially overlapping the big circle.

George might ask, "In Islam how are you taught to enter the kingdom?" The friend might describe the Five Pillars. Without commenting on those, George might mention a few verses about what Jesus said: It's a surrender of our will (Matt. 7:21), we can search for it (Matt. 13:45–46), and we must be born of the Spirit (John 3:3–5).

George might close the conversation by explaining that the Qur'an teaches that it's good to read the holy books. Would the friend like to learn more of what the Messiah has to say about the kingdom by reading some verses from the Qur'an and other holy books?

People who have learned this method from George have used it to great effect. One woman said she drew the circles in the shag carpet on the floor of her Pakistani neighbor's home. One sheikh in the Middle East explained the circles on his television show.

George has had many opportunities to speak about the kingdom with Muslims. Recently he had the chance to speak to Muslim leaders from a North African country. He explained Isa al-Masih's teaching about the kingdom of God. After George spoke, one of the imams went over each of George's points, agreed with each statement, and expanded on each point using verses from the Qur'an.

George said that as these kinds of seeds are sown, and the conversation centers on the message of Jesus, and as the person thinks more about what it means to enter the kingdom, the person of Jesus becomes more and more compelling. "I want to turn to Christ and Christ alone," George said. "A characteristic of the kingdom is that you and I have decided it's Jesus or nothing." As we move toward Jesus, we also move toward the main message of Jesus and the revolution that message can create.

Almost all of the people I met when I traveled talked about an inclusive process where people investigate the message of God, they start to obey God's teaching from the beginning, they form a centered set that moves toward the kingly reign of Jesus in their lives, they give their allegiance to Him, and they continue to grow as they study the Bible together with other people and put it into practice. For most of the people I talked to, this wasn't a controlled process, with a lot of outside direction. People were given time and space to explore at their own pace. They made changes in their lives and adjustments to their culture in their own ways.

This is where the last element comes in. How do people move along the continuum? How much outside influence do they receive?

Trusting the Holy Spirit

According to Carl, and most of the others I talked to, the answer isn't primarily found in the direction provided by experts like him. The answer is found in the Holy Spirit. Carl told me he would usually refuse to answer the questions put to him by the African farmers. He tried to keep his input to a minimum. He believed that God Himself would lead the believers as they discussed the Bible stories together. Carl called this process "community theologizing."

One day, after one of these jamaat groups read Acts 8, the jamaat leader said to Carl, "I want to be baptized and filled with the Spirit. That's what happened when Phillip went to Samaria and the apostles came down and prayed. People were baptized and filled with the Spirit. I want to go the whole way. I don't want anything to hold me back."

Carl responded, "This is wonderful. I think we need to discuss this."

The jamaat leader called together the leaders of the three other jamaats in the area. They discussed the question, Should we be baptized? One of them said, "Well, we can't get anywhere with baptism until we discuss funerals."

Carl laughed and said, "I would have never connected those thoughts."

The jamaat leaders realized that if they got baptized, their Muslim community might reject them. If that happened, when one of their loved ones died, maybe no one in the community would come to the funeral. That would bring shame on the family of the person who had died. The leaders came to the decision that they would support each other if there was a death in the family.

It took a year and a half before the jamaat leaders were ready for baptism. During this time they discovered what made them unique. Early on, they had considered how their convictions contrasted with the prevailing beliefs of the Muslims around them, and several of them had asked Carl, "What should we call ourselves? Who are we?" Carl replied, "I cannot answer that question for you. You've got to discover as a community through Scripture, through prayer, who God has called you to be."

After the community struggled through the issues of funerals and baptism, they also discovered what made them different and what might bring persecution on them. They realized it was their faith in Jesus. By uniting to do funerals together, they found their identity. "They were people who followed Jesus," Carl said, "and that's what made them different from the other Muslims."

Carl admitted that those eighteen months when the jamaat leaders were deciding whether to be baptized were scary for him. They could have decided not to be baptized. They could have developed a bizarre and damaging interpretation of this part of the Bible. But as he has trusted the Holy Spirit to guide the community through the Scriptures, "they have not developed any weird theology."

Roland Allen, a missionary to China, said that this kind of outcome shouldn't surprise us. Allen looked at the churches left behind by the apostle Paul, often after Paul had stayed in a city only a short time, and concluded that Paul believed in the Holy Spirit "not merely vaguely as a spiritual power, but as a Person indwelling His converts."[10] Therefore, Allen asserted, Paul must have trusted these people, not because of their own merits, but because he believed in the work of the Spirit in them.

Allen gave the example of how Paul dealt with the issue in Corinth of eating food that had been offered to idols. Allen noted that Paul didn't issue an edict, or appeal to the Jerusalem council, or even forbid the practice of attending feasts in the temple. Instead, Paul urged the Corinthians not to let their freedom become "a stumbling block to the weak."[11]

Paul risked making a mess by not providing a firmer rule. "St. Paul cannot have believed that by his appeal to charity the question would be settled," Allen insisted. "He must have foreseen strife and division. He must have deliberately preferred strife and division, heart-burnings, and distresses, and failures, to laying down a law."[12]

In his own day, Allen didn't see much evidence of Paul's approach. He saw instead policies, power structures, and control mechanisms put in place because of an "overcautious" fear of heresies and schisms. This fear, he wrote, had undermined faith in the Holy Spirit. He appealed for a return to Paul's methods.

"It would be better, far better," Allen argued, "that our converts should make many mistakes, and fall into many errors, and commit many offences, than that their sense of responsibility should be undermined. The Holy Ghost is given to Christians that He may guide them, and that they may learn His power to guide them, not that they may be stupidly obedient to the voice of authority."[13]

I think we still have a problem in this area today. Could an authority-oriented, bounded-set, labels-centered faith shrink a young person's sense of responsibility to seek first the kingdom in his or her life? I wondered that when I read a summary of the findings of the book *You Lost Me*.[14] In *You Lost Me*, David Kinnaman of the Barna Group presented the results of their research on people who were raised in the church but then left it after age fifteen.[15] Some left permanently and others left for an extended time. Reason number six given in the Barna Group report particularly caught my eye: "The church feels unfriendly to those who doubt."

Of the group surveyed, 36 percent said they did not feel "able to ask my most pressing life questions in church." Some of those questions must have been spiritual, because 26 percent admitted to having "significant intellectual doubts about my faith."

Have we created in our churches places where people don't feel comfortable journeying with us if they're not ready to agree with us? If young people don't think they belong "in," do they feel there is no other option than to be "out"? How and where can they ask their hard questions?

I believe that place might look like one that doesn't focus on labels or whether a person is in or out. One that doesn't emphasize answers from experts, but welcomes questions in the context of a group that looks to the Bible and trusts the Holy Spirit for answers to the mystery of how to live like one under the reign of Jesus. Maybe it would look a lot like Carl's jamaat.

In Thailand, as I rolled my suitcase over the polished tile that led to the exit of the resort, I passed several groups of people who were saying their good-byes. Carl was in one of those groups. When he saw me, he excused himself and hurried over to intercept me. "I hope I didn't give you the impression that we've got this all figured out," he told me. "It's very much a work in progress."

We talked briefly and I thanked him again for his time. As I rolled on and watched Carl walk back to his group, I thought, he's living what he teaches. He's putting this second principle into practice. He's trying to grow in his understanding of what it means to follow Christ, admitting he hasn't arrived, inviting many others to journey with him, trusting that in the midst of his discussions with others the Holy Spirit will help him and his friends grow and bear fruit. It's a principle that could help anyone live life deeper and wider.

10

Turn Pagan into Holy

Near the end of the classic TV program *A Charlie Brown Christmas*, Charlie Brown stands under a sparkling starry sky, clutching the little tree he had picked out for the Christmas pageant. He looks up, and the words Linus had spoken earlier come back to him: "For unto you is born this day, in the city of David, a Savior, which is Christ the Lord." Encouraged by these words, Charlie goes off to decorate his fragile possession. As he skips away, the sounds of the song "O Christmas Tree" accompany him.

In the middle of Christmas, this iconic TV show illustrates, the words of the angels wrap themselves around the needles of the evergreen. The Christmas trees and the Christmas carols—they seem made for each other.

Of course, many Americans have a vague understanding that the tree in the center of their family gatherings has a pagan background. The smell of pine needles in the home during the winter dates back to ancient times, when evergreen branches were seen as symbols of life. Roman families would decorate their homes with them in the new year. At roughly the same time, they would also celebrate Saturnalia, a festival in honor of Saturn, the god of agriculture. This feast began in the week leading up to December 21, winter solstice, and continued for a month afterward. In the middle of this celebration, many upper-class Romans also celebrated the birthday of Mithra, god of the sun, on December 25.[1]

In the year 350, in an effort to replace these winter festivities with a Christian holiday, Pope Julius I declared that December 25 would henceforth be celebrated as the birth of Jesus.

Eventually the evergreen became sanctified as well. The tree appeared as the "Paradise Tree" in medieval nativity plays. It was first decorated with round pastries as symbols of the Eucharist. In Germany those wafers became cookie ornaments.[2]

To the Puritans who settled in America, these heathen roots of Christmas were not acceptable. They didn't recognize the birth of Jesus on December 25, and, in fact, in Boston the celebration of Christmas was banned from 1659 to 1681. It wasn't until 1870 that Christmas finally became an official holiday in the United States.[3]

It's hard to imagine the unease of the Puritans now, when Christmas trees adorn church sanctuaries and Christmas itself has become a cherished part of the Christian calendar. As I traveled around the world, though, I saw the struggle of the Puritans in a new way. I met many new believers in Jesus trying to figure out what to do with the customs and holidays they had grown up with. Could they, like Julius I, take a day devoted to a god and turn it into a day honoring Jesus? If so, how?

I began to see this struggle as a third principle underlying the movements I witnessed. Most of the people I visited based their community life on discussions of Bible stories. They made room for people to obey Jesus all along their journey of faith. And they wrestled together with how to transform their customs into new ways of celebrating the truths of God. I started to believe that this principle could open doorways all across the world for people who have felt shut out from Jesus to come in and experience Him. The doorway of December 25 is just the beginning.

The Cremation

To give an idea of what this transition from pagan to holy looks like in our world today, I'd like to tell the story of the funeral of Navin's father.

I met Navin in a tiny office in India. Jay, the outreach team coordinator I met in India, had taken me to meet Navin, a slim, middle-aged Indian man wearing glasses and a baseball hat. We sat down and tried to cool off under the blast of a fan.

When Jay left to find us some cold drinks, Navin pulled out a map. Navin coordinates a team that has helped to start many Yeshu Bhakta fellowships in this city. He explained the colored dots on the map that showed where Jesus-centered satsangs have begun. When Jay returned, he asked Navin to tell me about his father's funeral.

Navin told me he grew up doing two kinds of puja, or worship: Hindu puja and Christian puja. His father was a Hindu and his mother was a Christian.

When Navin first got involved with Christian work, his Hindu father did not like it. When Navin got married, Navin made sure to serve only vegetarian food at the reception so his father and his other Hindu relatives would come. Eventually his father became attracted to the person of Jesus, but he didn't want to change his religion.

One year, the day after Christmas, Navin's father became very sick. In the evening he asked Navin to pray for him. "I felt concerned in my heart," Navin said. He explained to his father again about the importance of believing in Jesus. His father now was ready to make that commitment. "I led him in the sinner's prayer," Navin said.

That night, at about 11:00 p.m., his father died. That's when the son's dilemma began. In the midst of his grief, Navin had to decide, should we do the Christian way of burial or the Hindu style? He knew his mother wanted a Christian burial and his father would have wanted the Hindu cremation. Also his father's many Hindu friends and family would want to come and pay their respects. Navin and his wife prayed about what to do.

Navin was worried that as the son, he would be forced to chant the god Ram's name in the funeral ceremonies. Many Hindus chant Ram's name because they believe all truth is in Ram. They don't know what is going to happen in the reincarnation of this person, but they believe that all things are in Ram's hands, so they chant his name as they walk toward the burning site.

Navin also knew that the funeral is followed by a time of mourning, which involves many other Hindu rituals. For example, the family offers small cakes of rice once a day for ten days to help the deceased develop a new body. As the son, Navin knew he would be expected to carry out these necessary actions. The mourners would always look to him to see what he did.

He had never heard of a believer in Jesus participating in a Hindu cremation ceremony. He and his wife didn't have much time to figure out what they would do.

In spite of their concerns, they both sensed they should use the Hindu style. So Navin made arrangements for the funeral to begin the following morning. He thought, let's proceed and see what happens.

The next day, the Hindu mourners arrived. They washed the body and wrapped it in white cloth. They placed the body on a bamboo stretcher. A friend of Navin's read some verses from the Bible. Then Navin took one corner of the stretcher. Three other men each took their places around the body. Together, they lifted the stretcher up to their shoulders and began to make their way down the street toward the cremation site on the Ganges River. As they walked, people in the crowd began to chant, "*Ram Nam Satya Hai.*" They were saying, "The name of Ram is truth."

Navin was walking into uncharted territory. Could God be glori-
fied even in this Hindu cremation ceremony?

God and the Gods

It would seem unlikely, but many cherished parts of Christian
culture similarly came from heathen customs. The bridesmaids
at a Christian wedding, for example, were originally intended
as decoys for evil spirits, according to author John Davis. "They
were dressed the same as the bride in order to confuse the spirits
as to her real identity," Davis wrote.[4] The use of candles and
incense in churches was apparently inspired by Roman emperor
worship. In the book *Pagan Christianity?* Frank Viola reports that
when an emperor made a public appearance, servants would go
before him with torches and with a bowl of burning aromatic
spices. "Taking his cue from this custom," Viola wrote, "Constantine introduced candles and the burning of incense as part
of the church service. And they were brought in when the clergy
entered the room."[5]

Who would think one of the holiest days in the Christian year
would bear the name of a pagan goddess? Some scholars think the
name Easter originated from the name of the German goddess of
rebirth, Eostara. At the Feast of Eostara the gathered worshipers
celebrated the rebirth of earth and the rising of the spring sun.
According to author Steve Russo, "Two symbols for fertility—the
Easter bunny and eggs—are carryovers from this feast."[6]

How could Constantine, Julius I, and others take the trappings
of the gods and bring them into the worship of Jesus? Perhaps they
got their cue from the Bible itself.

From the beginning to the end of the Bible, God uses the language and imagery of the heathen world to communicate with
His people. After Abram arrived in the land God promised him,
he asked God to give him a sign to prove that he would indeed

become a great nation. Abram was an old man by now and still had no children. God responded by giving Abram a strange vision. In Genesis 15 God asked Abram to bring Him a heifer, a goat, a ram, a dove, and a pigeon. Abram did so, cutting the large animals in half and arranging the pieces opposite each other. When night fell, Abram saw a vision of a smoking firepot and a burning torch passing between the pieces. He also heard God speak to him, confirming His covenant.

According to the authors of *The IVP Bible Background Commentary*, this scene would have been full of meaning for Abram. In Aramaic and Hittite texts, passing between animals that had been sacrificed and cut in two would be a sign of purification or a ritual of making a treaty. As for the smoking firepot and flaming torch, censers and sacred torches were commonly used in nighttime Mesopotamian rituals of this period, such as rites of initiation or purification. They even symbolized the gods themselves. "While in Mesopotamia the torch and oven represented particular deities, here they represent Yahweh," the authors assert.[7]

Yahweh used symbols of pagan gods to represent Himself!

Similarly, when giving Abram a sign to demonstrate the covenant relationship between his community and Yahweh, God instituted a practice widely in use at that time. Circumcision already played a part in rites of puberty, fertility, and marriage.[8]

Not only did God use social customs, but He also took heathen religious practices for His own purposes. He used Balaam even though Balaam normally used sorcery to achieve his ends.[9] He used a star to guide astrologers. He sanctified all these methods for His own holy uses.

The followers of Jesus similarly filled existing concepts with new meanings. As they talked about their faith, they used terms that came from the polytheistic background of their day. "They took words from Greek philosophy, from pagan rites and pagan mysteries to express Christian concepts," wrote S. N. Wald. "In this way, words like *theos, kyrios, logos, soter, eulogia, mysterion, charis, prophetia, baptismos, episcopos, diaconos* were taken to express specific Christian ideas."[10]

Today many Christians think of this process of assimilating pagan culture as something that happened many years ago. It can seem somewhat irrelevant to the issues we face in our modern world. But the decisions Navin faced at the death of his father show that this process is still acutely important and personal for many people all over the planet.

As Navin and the others got closer to the Ganges, they began going down steps toward the haze of smoke ahead of them. Navin could hear the chants *"Ram Nam Satya Hai"* around him. He either said nothing or inserted Yeshu's name in the chant. *"Yeshu Nam Satya Hai,"* Navin declared. "The name of Jesus is truth."

When the mourners got to the burning site and looked out at the wide expanse of the river, they put the body down. Navin had to buy wood and *ghee,* clarified butter. The ghee would be used to light the wood. And Navin had to buy the fire. The men who work at this cremation site say the funeral fire has been burning for four thousand years and Shiva himself lit the fire. The family of the deceased has to buy a piece of the fire.

Then one of Navin's nephews had to walk around the body counterclockwise three times with the fire. When he finished, the nephew lit the wood underneath the body. As the sticks crackled and began to blaze, Navin turned his back on the fire and made his way up the steps away from the river. He and the others were supposed to walk away and not look back. Navin admitted he did look back.

On the tenth day after the cremation, Navin shaved his head as a traditional sign of mourning. During the thirteen-day mourning period, however, there were parts of the ceremonies Navin and his wife didn't do, like offering the rice cakes. They also changed some parts of the rituals. For example, during the days of mourning, a *havan,* or fire ceremony, is sometimes used. But Navin and his wife put candles in the windows to symbolize that Jesus is the light of the world. Also Navin was supposed to offer water by pouring it through his hands using a sacred grass called *kusa*. But Navin and his wife prayed these words every day: "Let living water flow from here."

In spite of these changes, Navin's Hindu family members were pleasantly surprised that Navin had done the cremation and the mourning in the Hindu style. Not expecting this, some had first gone to a Christian burial site to look for Navin and his family there, then heard they had gone to the burning house on the Ganges.

Navin's pastor, though, was upset. When he visited Navin after the funeral, the pastor asked why Navin had shaved his head. "I love my father," Navin told him. "I'm in a time of mourning for him."

"It's not in the Bible that we should shave our head," the pastor stated.

Navin didn't want to argue. He said, "Okay. Maybe show me in the Bible where it is written that shaving the head is a sin."

"He couldn't show me," Navin said.

The discomfort of the pastor and the concerns of Navin himself show that the process of putting new meaning into a practice that used to convey unbiblical ideas is a journey with perils on every side. When people like Navin try to remake a ceremony like the Hindu cremation rituals, they don't want erroneous ideas to remain. They don't want other believers to think, for example, that the chief mourner is purified by the removal of his hair. They also don't want to add new legalisms to faith. They don't want believers to think that if the chief mourner doesn't walk three times around a dead body the family can't be sure their loved one will spend eternity in heaven.

Jesus said that outward religious rituals can't make a person clean. He also said that traditions can prevent people from following God.[11] Religious customs, if improperly used, can become control mechanisms, can divert attention away from the Bible, can hinder change, can create cliques, can become rote, and can create a false sense of security (see the rich young ruler in Luke 18:21).

Yet, if properly used, traditions can provide a sense of identity, a way of blessing members of a group, and can provide shared memories, spiritual growth, comfort, and a format for worship and celebration.

The apostle Paul, in his letters to the small groups of believers who were trying to live out their faith in the polytheistic world of their day, often commented on these issues. The Galatian believers, for example, faced pressure to live according to Jewish traditions. To them, Paul wrote, "It is for freedom that Christ has set us free. Stand firm, then, and do not let yourselves be burdened again by a yoke of slavery."[12]

The people I met on my travels told me they were aware of the dangers of traditions becoming empty legalistic obligations. On the other hand, they told me the cultures I was visiting didn't separate the sacred and the secular. In Hindu and Buddhist cultures, for example, the concept of religion is very broad. Hindus use the word *dharma* to refer to the outworking of their faith. As Jay explained it to me, "Dharma doesn't mean religion as we understand it. Dharma is your whole social community with all your duties according to your life as a family member, to your community, to your job. Dharma is your entire holistic life."

For most of the world, there's no question that following God is meant to involve all of life. If customs, traditions, and rituals don't become part of that, the person feels adrift, floating away from their homeland. A lack of sensitivity in this area has been one of the main reasons so much of the world has not discovered a way to follow Jesus.

The people I met who came from a Western culture and were working in non-Western places mostly emphasized that they wanted the local people to figure out on their own what to do with their cultural setting. In some cases, workers I met wanted to help people, such as Japanese or Native Americans who had been told their culture was bad, to reconsider how their former traditions could be redeemed. If we put flowers on graves in the West, why can't

Japanese believers in Jesus do something to show respect to their ancestors? If we use big drum sets in Western churches, why can't Native Americans also use the drum?

These two examples show an underlying hypocrisy in some of the Christian opposition to the redemption of other cultures. We have a history in Western Christianity of adopting and sanctifying pagan customs, but often we haven't let Asian, African, or tribal cultures find a way to adapt their own festivals and traditions.

I see two main problems with this. First, the Christian world has missed out on the richness of rituals that could enhance our faith. Second, and most significantly, a lack of these customs means a lack of pathways to Jesus.

Opening Doorways

While traveling, I often asked the people I met how their experiences have helped them spiritually. Several times Western people talked about Eastern customs they now cherish in their own life.

In India, for example, I visited the home of a young family from the United States. After chatting with Scott in the living room, his wife, Amy, came in to greet us. She was an attractive woman wearing a *shalwar kameez*, the flowing shirt, scarf, and trousers common across India. In her arms, she was holding her one-year-old son, Drew. I noticed that Drew's head was almost bald. Later, Scott explained that he and Amy had recently gone through the Hindu hair cutting ceremony called *mundan*.

Scott and Amy work with a small community of Hindu Yeshu Bhaktas. As a sign of respect for the culture, and after a lot of consultation with their Indian friends, they decided to have a mundan ceremony for Drew. In this ritual, performed shortly after the child's first birthday, family, friends, and a Hindu priest gather in a home or temple. The priest recites mantras, he kindles a holy fire, and together with the father or an uncle, he cuts four small locks of hair from each side of the child's head. After this, a barber completely shaves the child's hair. According to author Shukavak Dasa, the parents sacrifice the beauty of their son or daughter and "in exchange they ask God for long life and prosperity for their child."[13]

Scott and Amy invited a Christ-following man who comes from a pundit's (priest's) family to do the ceremony. They didn't invite everyone in the fellowship to the event because, Scott said, "We didn't know exactly how it would go." As they cut Drew's locks, they offered prayers to God for him.

Both Scott and Amy found it a significant experience. "It was very meaningful to us," Amy told me later. Scott said it helped them better understand the culture and feelings of the disciples they had come to love.

I wondered if others might find inspiration from the mundan ceremony to help them dedicate their child to God.

Mark and Emily, a couple I met in Thailand, actually brought one Buddhist ceremony home with them. At Thai New Year, young people traditionally go to older friends or family members whom they want to bless, such as parents, aunts, or grandparents. They pour water over the hands of the older person and offer a blessing. Then the older person returns the blessing. When Mark and Emily went back to their home country in the West, they wanted to do something to honor an older Baptist couple who had been praying for them. They decided to use this Thai form of blessing. They poured the water over their friends' hands and prayed for them. "They found that really meaningful," Emily told me.

It might seem strange to think Christians in the West would shave their child's head or pour water over the hands of their grandparents. But who would think we would go into the woods, cut down an evergreen, and prop it up in our living room? Now this custom carries a lot of meaning. Maybe other traditions could bring similar vitality to our lives.

We don't have to be limited by the cultural box that faith in Christ now finds itself in. If we're led by the Bible and by a sincere desire for Jesus to be the center of our lives, we can discover how to redeem our own pagan practices or learn from the traditions of other cultures.

So my first point is, going from pagan to holy can enrich us.

Second, and most important, this method can provide a doorway to Jesus for many people who feel disconnected from Christian culture. December 25, the birthday of Mithra, has provided a doorway to Jesus for millions of people. What other doorways could we make so that people in our world today would feel free to seek Jesus?

I read a story about a Youth With A Mission team in England that set up a "Creation Prayer" booth at the Body Mind Spirit festival in London. This New Age event, which attracts thousands of people at different venues in Europe and North America, bills itself as a showcase for "innovation in the world of natural healing and spiritual growth." At their booth, the YWAM team offered a form of prayer in which they asked God to give them understanding about God's original design for the person. Over six days, they prayed for more than four hundred people at the stand.

One day a woman named Gail came for prayer. A young lady, Dondi Carter, prayed for Gail. As Dondi spent some time in silence, she got a picture in her mind of Gail surrounded by boxes. In the scene, Gail was crying out for help and didn't know what to do. Dondi asked Gail if that picture meant anything to her. Gail said her whole house was filled with boxes at the moment. She had just gotten a divorce. She said she wished she had the ability to talk to God as Dondi and the others were doing. By the end of their talk, Dondi prayed with Gail and Gail decided to follow Christ.

As Gail was leaving, she said, "For eight or nine years, I have been searching for something, trying all these different things. Who would have thought the answer was so simple as Jesus?"[14]

For Gail, her ritual of going to the Body Mind Spirit festival seeking spiritual experiences led her to a doorway at the Creation Prayer booth. At that prayer stand, all they really had to offer was biblical faith in Jesus. But through this unique doorway, Gail was able to see what she hadn't seen growing up around Christian churches in England. Somehow the festivals and words of New Age culture helped her recognize what had always been right in front of her nose.

What other rituals or customs from our modern world could also provide doorways to Jesus? For me, it's a fascinating thought, and one deserving of a lot of experimentation.

For Navin, his willingness to step out into the midst of a Hindu ceremony, carrying his father's body on his shoulder, provided a doorway to Jesus for many of his family members.

On the thirteenth day after the Hindu cremation activities, the bereaved family gives food to relatives, friends, and neighbors. Navin did this too. Many of his Hindu relatives came to visit him. Some came from quite a distance away. They were all intrigued to find out why Navin, as a follower of Jesus, had honored their Hindu traditions. They asked him many questions about his beliefs and invited him to visit them and explain more.

"They were very happy," Navin said. "They know we follow Jesus in a Hindu way."

11

Seek the Whole Truth

Does a story about the god Vishnu, taken from the Hindu scriptures, belong as the centerpiece of a Sunday morning sermon in a Christian church? Apparently Jay, the man I visited in India, thought so.

I had come to a conference at Redeemer Lutheran Church in Minneapolis at which Jay was one of the speakers. He had been asked to lead the contemporary service on Sunday.

The church in which Jay was speaking couldn't have fit in better with suburban America. The sprawling brick complex was surrounded by a subdivision. Across the street sat tidy houses with neat lawns. On this May morning, pink and yellow tulips brightened the flower beds by the doors of the church.

Inside, Jay sat on a stage draped in Indian cloth. Around him the members of the band Aradhna also sat on the stage, each with an instrument. Everyone wore Indian clothing. The band's vocalist, Chris Hale, wore a blue kurta and held a sitar.

Jay was talking about stories. "In the West," he said, "we have lots of points in church. We punish people with multiple subpoints and different systematic outlines, and then we add in a few stories, which are what the people really want to hear. In India we tell stories, and the story itself is the point. Out of the story, you draw analogies to a person's life."

He had already explained that he wanted to use a satsang format for the service. Aradhna had led the congregation in a bhajan song. Jay had told a couple of stories from his work in India. Chris had also sung a chant in Sanskrit. He gave the translation:

> Lead me from falsehood to truth,
> from darkness to light.
> Lead me from death to everlasting light.

Now Jay got into his central story. "One time there was a king, a forest king," he said. He was an elephant named Gajendra. One hot day, the elephant went to cool off at a lake. His wives and the other forest creatures joined him.

"All of a sudden, *bang!* A crocodile grabbed his leg," Jay exclaimed. The crocodile tried to pull Gajendra into the lake. Gajendra pulled back. They struggled like this for a thousand years.

"Everything in the Hindu world is a thousand," Jay explained. "That means either too much or a very long time." The crowd in the auditorium laughed.

Gajendra asked the forest creatures and his wives to help him. Even with their help, he couldn't pull himself free of the crocodile. Finally, as Gajendra's strength was about to run out, he thought of calling out to the Almighty. As soon as he cried out for mercy, a disc came flying through the air. It cut the crocodile in half. Gajendra pulled himself free. He thanked the Almighty.

Jay said, "The Almighty said to him, 'I watched you from the very first day. The minute you call upon my name, you will be saved.'"

The crocodile represents sin, Jay explained. "The crocodiles of lust, the crocodiles of bitterness, the crocodiles of lack of self-control, these affect us all and we can't get away from them. We can't extract ourselves, and our friends can't help us. Only when we throw ourselves on the mercy and grace of Sadguru Yeshu, of Jesus Christ, can we be taken out of that situation."

In his explanation, Jay left out the fact that the Almighty in the original story was Vishnu, not Jesus. He also didn't say that the story comes from the Bhagavata Purana, one of the Hindu scriptures. In fact, on a Hindu website, the writer tells the story of Gajendra and then makes the following application: "One should meditate upon the Lord Vishnu . . . who has four arms . . . for removal of all obstacles."[1]

Not everyone I met on my travels would use stories from other religions to teach about Jesus as Jay did. But I did encounter an openness to learn from other faiths. This practice was so widespread that I began to recognize it as a fourth foundational principle of the movements I studied. I started to believe that this principle also has power to break barriers—to welcome and affirm people from a variety of backgrounds, and to revitalize and enlarge the faith of any believer. I heard this principle expressed in at least two main ways:

- Discover God's truth, even in other religions.
- Stay curious.

Like the other boundary breakers, this principle comes from the teachings of the Bible.

Discover God's Truth, Even in Other Religions

Two young men went to pagan schools, studied about the gods, and emerged the better for it. One of these men I met. The other I read about.

The one I met was lying on a hospital bed in India. A friend of his took me to see him. When we arrived at the hospital, a receptionist behind a metal grate told us what room he was in. We walked through dark hallways, past a courtyard, and up stairs. We found Jose Joseph in a room with blue walls. He lay on a bed with an IV hooked to his arm. Two fans blew on him. Joseph explained that he had been exhausted and sick with the flu. He hoped this IV treatment at the hospital would revive him. I found out later this practice of getting IV fluids is fairly common in India.

Joseph, a bald, muscular man, still had enough strength to tell me his story. He grew up in a Christian family in South India. From an early age, he displayed a talent for singing. By the time he was four years old, he was already singing with a Christian music team, traveling to many cities in India. As a young adult, he participated in evangelistic drama and dance in Nepal.

Joseph saw how the arts made the gospel message clear to the crowds who gathered around them. He decided to learn more about the arts, particularly the art forms of his own country. He decided to enroll in a Hindu music school.

This plan didn't make his family very happy. They said, "You are a born-again Christian. How can you go and study in a Hindu music academy?" They warned Joseph he would have to sing Hindu songs.

Joseph realized they were trying to protect him. They didn't want him to lose his faith. He knew it was a valid concern. "This music is so rich," he said. "It has a power to attract people."

When Joseph joined the college, he discovered that out of seven hundred students he was the only Christian. He studied there for four years. "All my friends were Brahmins, the high-caste people," he said. "They were very talented."

To learn the traditional music genre Joseph wanted to focus on, called *Carnatic* music, Joseph had to sing worship songs using the names of the Hindu gods. Asking Jesus to protect him, he would sing with prayers to God in his heart. "You need to have a deep relationship with Jesus, first of all," he emphasized.

Joseph emerged from the school with his faith intact. Many of his fellow classmates went on to become professional singers. They now sing on TV and in big Hindu classical productions.

Joseph began to explore how to use his classical training as part of his faith in Jesus.

A few years after he graduated, he met a man who gave him an image that guided and inspired him. This man had grown up in an Indian Muslim family but later became a Christian. The man talked to Joseph about the story in which Jesus asks the disciples to cast the net on the other side of the boat.[2] This man made the point that in India after two thousand years of telling people about Jesus, still less than 6 percent had become Christians.[3] "Maybe we need to fish in the deeper part," the man said.

Joseph realized, "The deep side of India is our culture." In the music, the dance, the drama, the history, Joseph told me, India has deep roots. He said Bollywood has tapped into that. It's why Indian movies have to have three or four songs and dances. Christians, though, haven't caught on to this, Joseph claimed. They "haven't got to the deeper part of India."

This idea about the deeper part helped Joseph visualize what he'd been thinking about for so long. "I said, 'God, that is the revelation I've been looking for all these years. I have got it and I will do it.'"

Since then, he has worked hard to put that vision into action. He leads a ministry that includes a bhajan team, a rock band, a traditional dance troupe, a recording studio, and a training program for worship leaders. He has had several opportunities to bring traditional art forms into big Christian gatherings.

Joseph told me his four years of music study, which also included instruction in Sanskrit and Indian history, took him only to a surface level of the music in his culture. He intends to continue studying. "It's lifetime learning," he said.

The man I read about went through a similar journey. He also went to a school where he learned about gods and their powers. He was even given a new name, a name that proclaimed he was a "prince" of one of the gods.[4] After many years, he also came out of his school with his faith still intact. He had drawn the line early on between what violated his core beliefs and what he could enter into, but he did not reject the pagan learning environment. He dedicated himself to gain all the wisdom he could gather, applying himself to every matter of wisdom and understanding available in his new school.

This man emerged as one of the top students. He was found to be ten times wiser than the magicians and enchanters. As a result, he was named leader of the magicians and astrologers, who specialized in exorcism of demons and the divination of dreams.[5]

He was given the name Belteshazzar, but his original name was Daniel. As one of the Jews captured in 597 BC, Daniel was picked to go to a royal training school in the center of the Chaldean kingdom. He studied in a city that worshiped the god Marduk, considered the chief of all the gods.[6]

Daniel's studies seemed to strengthen his spiritual gifts and his natural intelligence. His devotion to Yahweh, if anything, seemed to grow stronger.

He could use the Persian term, God of Heaven, to describe God. This was a name commonly used for Ahura Mazda, the main deity of Zoroastrianism.[7] Daniel recognized that God had been active in Babylonian society long before Daniel ever arrived.[8] This recognition led him to say that God Himself had given King Nebuchadnezzar authority.

Daniel's understanding of Chaldean spiritual practices seemed to give him more confidence to point to the great God. He knew the limits of what enchanters and diviners could do, and he knew that what God was revealing to him surpassed it all.[9]

Many years later, in the midst of another vast empire, both Jesus and the apostle Paul could also affirm the value of learning from people who followed other religions. Not only did Jesus use the faith of a Roman military commander as an example for the Jews, but he also pointed back in history to similar examples of people from nations around Israel, nations that did not follow Yahweh, who exhibited faith that they as the people of God could still learn from.[10] He spoke about a widow in Sidon, and Naaman, a Syrian.[11]

Similarly, the apostle Paul, in an effort to communicate to the educated elite of Athens, appealed to the insight of a person who followed a non-Jewish religion. He quoted from a well-known poet, a man who wrote about the god Zeus. The poem reads:

> They fashioned a tomb for you, holy and high one,
> Cretans, always liars, evil beasts, idle bellies.
> But you are not dead: you live and abide forever,
> For in you we live and move and have our being.[12]

Paul, who had not only read this pagan poem but had also carefully studied the statues of gods in the city of Athens, said that this God they had called the unknown god was not a distant god. "He is not far from any one of us," Paul declared. "'For in him we live and move and have our being.'"[13]

By using an excerpt from a poem about Zeus, Paul felt free to take what was true out of what the poet Epimenides wrote. The "him" in that poem referred to Zeus. But if a follower of Jesus lives and moves and has his or her being in God, then Epimenides conveyed a truth, even though he was writing about Zeus. Paul wasn't agreeing with everything Epimenides wrote, just with that part, as it reflected the character of God. In that way it was true, and Paul could use it.[14]

Three hundred years later, Augustine endorsed this practice of using truth no matter where one discovers it, saying, "A person who is a good and true Christian should realize that truth belongs to his Lord, wherever it is found, gathering and acknowledging it even in pagan literature, but rejecting superstitious vanities. . . ."[15] In other words, "All truth is God's truth."

Similarly, many of the people I met on my travels would look around them and find truths that they could benefit from. Rather than approaching their environment as heathen and appalling, they viewed themselves as learners.

In Muslim communities, for example, many followers of Jesus I met would not speak disrespectfully of Muhammad. Instead, they affirmed the truths Muhammad proclaimed about God. In this, they followed the pattern of the pioneer missionary Samuel Zwemer, who wrote in 1912, "To help our Muslim brethren to answer this question [who is Jesus?], we must . . . lead them up to higher truth by admitting all of the truth which they possess."[16]

In *Mere Christianity*, C. S. Lewis gave a broad endorsement of this kind of approach. "If you are a Christian," he wrote, "you are free to think that all these religions, even the queerest ones, contain at least some hint of truth."[17]

It's a truth we can use, because it's God's truth. In fact, it's a truth that can help us understand more of God. In his book *Can Evangelicals Learn from World Religions?*, professor Gerald McDermott explains how people who believe in Christ can benefit from other religions. An expert on the theologian Jonathan Edwards, McDermott teaches religion at a college in Virginia. That role has led him into a deeper study of world religions. As he was exposed to the teachings of other faiths, he found himself growing in his own understanding of the Bible.

He writes, for example, that through Buddhist and Daoist teachings, he has grasped more of what it means to have union with Christ. Buddhists teach about letting go of what they call "desire." They talk about relinquishing self-centered thoughts and intentions. As he reflected on this Buddhist idea of letting go, McDermott came to a greater understanding of what the apostle Paul calls "putting off the old self."[18] Paul's concept of dying with Christ, wrote McDermott, involves "a letting go that allows the life of Christ to mysteriously rise up within us. It's the losing of our lives that results in the finding of our true lives."[19] Buddhist and Daoist teachings helped McDermott understand this idea better. He didn't start to believe differently from what Christians have traditionally believed about Paul's teaching on the old self and the new self. He just encountered new ideas that formed an "extension" of Paul's concept.[20]

McDermott makes the limitations of other religions clear. "There may exist revelations *from* God in other religions, but only in the religion of the Christ is there the revelation *of* God as incarnate in Jesus of Nazareth."[21]

But McDermott encourages believers in Jesus to search for more illumination, not only from the pages of the Bible, but even from the sacred writings of other faiths. "If Jesus counseled His disciples to learn from pagans about faith and God," McDermott concludes, "it seems arbitrary to rule out any new understanding coming from consideration of non-Christian traditions."[22]

We can benefit from God's truth wherever we find it, even if we find it in other religions.

Stay Curious

In chapter 9 I mentioned a study done by the Barna Group that gives one of the reasons young people who were raised in the church have left their faith. They don't think the church is a safe place to talk about their doubts. Commenting on the participants in the study, David Kinnaman wrote, "Many feel that they have been offered slick or half-baked answers to their thorny, honest questions and they are rejecting the 'talking heads' and 'talking points' they see among the older generations."[23]

An earlier Barna study, which focused on young people who remain outside the church, came to a similar conclusion. "Outsiders told us that the underlying concern of Christians often seems more about being right than about listening," Kinnaman reported.[24]

I've heard this kind of attitude for myself and from myself. Early one morning I had breakfast with a friend at a neighborhood restaurant. I couldn't help overhearing a man talking loudly at a table near me. He and the young man sitting opposite him had finished their eggs and were having a Bible study. As the older man expounded on the significant parts of the Scripture passage, he hardly stopped to take a breath. Occasionally he would become aware that the younger man wasn't talking. He would ask what his friend thought. Then he would begin again.

I had to admire the man's enthusiasm for the Bible. But he was so confident in everything he was saying. There wasn't much room for discussion. I cringed listening to him because I thought of all the times I've sounded the same. My smug self-assurance in what I believe has radiated out when I've spoken to groups, to my children, and to my own friends over breakfast.

The apostle Paul has a warning for people like me. "Knowledge puffs up while love builds up," Paul wrote. "Those who think they know something do not yet know as they ought to know."[25]

This principle—seek the whole truth—breaks boundaries because it brings a humility that welcomes others. We're all seekers after truth, no matter what part of the journey we're on. None of us have arrived. We can all say to anyone, to the young woman with Down syndrome, to the Hindu sadhu with ash on his forehead, to the Buddhist monk with his alms bowl: "Come and share your insights with me."

We're not saying we know nothing. We're just saying we don't know everything.

Author H. L. Richard, when advising people who want to make friendships with Hindus, emphasizes this essential quality. "Be quick to acknowledge mystery and lack of full understanding," Richard advises. "The greatest of thinkers know almost nothing about God, and the Hindu appreciates those who have a deep sense of the mystery of God and life."[26]

Increasingly, science can help us develop this teachable curiosity. The new generation has grown up with new science, which has humbled even the greatest minds. Relativity, quantum mechanics, chaos theory, and the uncertainty principle have turned upside down previously accepted conclusions. One M.I.T.–trained physicist commented, "There is not one thing in physics I am absolutely sure of."[27]

Both science and religion, it seems, face the same dangers and the same opportunities. In both cases, we can get stuck thinking we've got everything figured out. Science and religion together fight a "tireless battle against skepticism and dogmatism, against unbelief and superstition," wrote Max Planck, one of the originators of quantum theory. He said the goal is "toward God!"[28]

We fight against the dogmatic certainty that we have nothing left to learn. We grasp for new revelations wherever we can find them. In the process, we discern a bit more clarity about the nature of God, and we can find ourselves increasingly welcoming the insights of others and entering more into dialogue and less into monologue.

At the end of the service in Minneapolis, Jay tried to encourage the crowd to do as he'd done. After giving his lesson from the Hindu scriptures, Jay asked the audience to think of anyone they knew from an Indian or Hindu background. He urged them to think about how they could hear their friend's songs, how they could share stories of Jesus with their friends, and how they could learn from their friend's experiences. As a starting point, he said they could learn some Jesus-centered bhajans, like the ones we had sung that morning, and share them with their friends.

He told the crowd we would sing one last bhajan together. "I'd like you to come and lay your shoes at the altar for this person as a symbolic gesture that you care about them."

Chris Hale of Aradhna explained that we were going to sing the song "*Amrit Vani*," which he said means "Your Immortal Word."

As we stood and began to sing, the young lady in front of me took off her shoes and brought them to the front. The song went faster and faster. We were clapping and singing verses that praised the Father, the Spirit, and the Son: "*Jai jai Yeshu, Jai Jai ho*" (victory, victory be to Jesus, victory, victory).[29]

At the end, sixteen pairs of shoes, including two orange sandals, formed a ragged line at the bottom of the stage. A young man who seemed to be the pastor bounded up the steps to the platform. He looked in wonder at the shoes. He said, "God has placed redemptive stories in each culture, and we need to unlock those."

The boundary breaker principle number four—seek the whole truth—can demolish barriers to learning, and barriers to relationship. Taken together with the other principles—put the Book in its place; move toward Jesus; and turn pagan into holy—it can open the way for people to find Jesus, and for Jesus-followers to experience new vitality in their lives.

What would happen if these principles got stirred up in a pot together? What new fragrances might we smell here in the Western world? What formats for worship might grow and blossom? What doorways to Jesus might people create?

After I returned from my trips to Asia, I began to hunt for examples of these principles in action. One of my first stops took me to a yoga studio in California.

Part Three

LIVING BEYOND
BORDERS

12

Outside the Bun

In a 2002 commercial, a young man watching a kung fu movie rubs his sleepy eyes, gets up, and pulls a frosty hot dog from the freezer. He plops it in a microwave, punches the start button, and watches as his dinner thaws and then explodes, spewing shards of hot dog everywhere. Just then, on the young man's TV, a Buddhist monk, hands pressed together, says, "Cheer up, my son. Taco Bell is open late, so spice up your night with the grilled, stuffed burrito." The camera cuts to a close-up of the monk's serious face. "When it is late," he counsels, "think outside the bun."

That tag line "Think outside the bun," which Taco Bell used in its commercials for at least seven years, captures for me what the fellowships I visited are getting at. It even pictures what I think could happen to people's faith in Jesus around the world.

I introduced this idea in chapter 2. In some ways, I picture Christian culture like the hamburger. It's mostly a Western creation. It has some varieties, like guacamole–pepper jack, or gruyère-bacon-aioli-arugula, but it's pretty much the same from place to place. I picture the spread of Christian culture around the world like the proliferation of McDonald's franchises. Yes, McDonald's provides nonbeef options in India, but basically it offers the American burger under the Golden Arches in every country.

Christian culture has spread through the same kind of franchise method. Historically, the denominations and agencies have not encouraged much flavor variation in their exports to India or Africa. Around the world, we have preachers standing in churches, speaking to audiences sitting in rows, and the audience mostly doesn't talk back. Some people, like me, grew up on that diet and still enjoy it. Others, especially more and more of the Millennial generation, crave something else.

What could it mean to think outside of this bun? What if we could import something that tastes different? As Africans, Indians, and Chinese work out their faith without the pressure to adopt Western formats, they are creating their own flavors of biblical Jesus-following. They, and people like them from other continents, are allowing the Holy Spirit to speak to them as they study the Bible together. They are pursuing the central goal of Christlikeness and Christ's kingdom. They are finding ways for the worship of Jesus to emerge even from pagan origins. And they are pursuing God-given truth wherever they find it. Their principles, and their discoveries, can give us new vitality as well.

I'd like to invite you to envision some ways in which those discoveries can make faith more nourishing and more appetizing for you and for the people in your neighborhood. Imagine you've come with me to an Indian restaurant for the lunchtime buffet. I push open the jingling door. As we step inside, we smell the fragrance of cumin, cardamom, and coriander. We see Bollywood dancers gyrating on a flat-screen TV in the corner. Along the wall in front of us, steam rises from dozens of dishes now hidden under the warming lights. I invite you to come with me through the buffet of new flavors. There are many I've never experienced before, and I don't know the names that are scrawled on little tags above them. But I'll suggest four for you to put on your plate.

Use New Words

The musical group Aradhna performs in two worlds. They have sung bhajans about Jesus in Hindu temples. They have also brought a Hindu tabla drummer with them to concerts in Christian churches. Chris Hale, the lead vocalist for the band, admits he has often struggled to find a common identity in these two settings.

At one church where Aradhna played, the missions pastor and other speakers repeatedly talked about the good news of Jesus for Hindus. Eventually Anand, the tabla player, got up and quietly walked out. Concerned, Hale followed him and asked Anand if anything was wrong. Anand said, "It's okay. I'm not really upset. I understand that is what these people believe, but honestly, I just want to stand up and tell them, 'We Hindus have good news for you too.'"[1]

At a Hindu temple, as Aradhna was doing a sound check, an old man gestured to all the carved figures around the room and asked Aradhna's violin player, "Do you like my gods?"

Hale says he is learning how to speak about himself when in the presence of both Christians and Hindus. As a musician who grew up in a boarding school in India, then studied music at Berklee College of Music in Boston, and who also earned the Visharad degree in sitar in India, Hale has had many opportunities to wrestle with these questions. How can he avoid living a dual life, being one person to Hindus and another to Christians?

Hale says he is trying to live in a way that is truer and more real. "I am seeking . . . to adopt a vocabulary and behavior that is the same everywhere I go. One that is far more 'Christian' among Hindus, and far more 'Hindu' among Christians, rather than a lukewarm version of myself that might be acceptable to both."[2]

Rick Love, who worked among Muslims for twenty-five years, would say that Hale has been finding his core message. Love calls this search "3D communication." He says believers in Jesus increasingly have to communicate with three different audiences: the followers of other faith traditions, secular people, and Christians. On a blog or a website, for example, all three of these groups could read what believers write. Love believes it's possible to boldly use the same words when talking to a Muslim, a church leader, or a secular journalist.

It's not about coming up with a slick public relations veneer. It's first of all about clarifying a person's core message. Love suggests believers ask themselves, "What am I willing to die for?"

Love recommends sharing this message openly, as Jesus did, but also carefully considering the meanings of the words we use.[3] If we think about how our message will fall on the ears of a Buddhist monk or a secular businessman, we can sometimes discover words and phrases that no longer mean what we want them to mean. To one of these people, words like "missionary," "evangelism," and "convert" might imply manipulation to force a change from one religion to another. Is that what we mean when we use these words?

In response to this concern, Love has found different language to express these missionary or evangelistic concepts. He uses what he calls "blessing the nations" terminology. These words originate in the calling of Abram and extend to the language of Paul.[4] "Thus," suggests Love, "our core message is blessing in Christ and our core mandate is blessing all nations."[5] Love can use this blessing language with a secular neighbor, a Christian at church, or a Muslim in Indonesia.

Could it be that one thing that turns people off from biblical faith is the use of cliché words that no longer convey the message we intend? Could these automatic phrases also keep our own thinking stale?

I wonder if the movements I've studied, as they have often chosen not to use the word "Christian" because of the way the word is misunderstood in their context, can prod us to rethink the meaning of our other spiritual words.

One day, while sitting in a Pakistani restaurant, I talked to my friend Kristin about this. By the age of twenty-four, Kristin, a graduate of Moody Bible Institute, had already worked with hippies in India and street people in Israel. We got on the subject of how to speak to young people in the West who don't connect with the Christian faith. We thought about two groups of kids, those who grow up in the church and become disenfranchised, and those who never experience Christianity at all. How can we use words that will reach them?

"Both of them need to hear Jesus communicated in a way other than 'I got saved' or 'I asked Jesus into my heart' or 'You need to grow in Christ,'" Kristin observed. "They need to hear truth communicated with different vocabulary."

A pastor I met, Buddy Hoffman of Grace Fellowship Church in Snellville, Georgia, found a new vocabulary as he tried to do something to bless the Muslim world. After 9/11, he led teams that tried unsuccessfully to communicate with Muslims in Afghanistan, London, and Iraq. Then he met people who were using a different approach. They were using kingdom circles, and they approached the Qur'an with respect.

This discovery finally helped Hoffman and his congregation build friendships with Muslims overseas. Their success led Hoffman to start thinking about teens in Snellville. Could they also benefit from a different vocabulary? Hoffman's son asked him, "How do we announce the kingdom to this generation?"

Inspired by how Jesus's kingdom language took words of day-to-day living, like mustard seeds and coins and birth, to cause people to think about deeper questions, they have tried to do the same with youth in the Atlanta area. They have asked questions like, "Why is it that we're attracted to beauty?"

An editor I know suggests that even other religions can give us words. Rebecca Cooper, a former editor at Baker Publishing, told me that she sometimes finds the wording of Buddhism helpful. "There are so many Buddhist sayings and teachings that could have come straight out of Jesus's mouth," she said. She gave examples of Jesus's teachings on compassion, patience, or not wasting time on worry. She said somehow when she hears similar points in new language, she can pay attention to these concepts in a new way. "Because I grew up with the Christian phrasing," Rebecca explained, "the Buddhist presentation of these same ideas makes them feel fresh and not clichéd."

When I met with Kristin over lunch, she also suggested looking to modern-day musicians who have gotten beyond purely secular themes. What words do they use? If these lyrics contain truth, we can use that truth the way the apostle Paul used the words of a well-known poet from his day.

I pressed Kristin for some specifics. She mentioned the vocalist of one popular group who said, "Our music captures joy." She thought of using words that imply spirituality beyond religion, like "energy" and "presence."

Kristin talked about how the translation of the Bible led to the spread of faith in Jesus around the world. Maybe it's time for another kind of translation effort, Kristin suggested. It's time for the translation of our own words. It's time to find words that convey our real meaning in a way that people outside our Christian culture can understand.

Meet in New Places

At 7:00 in the evening on a train rattling along from Bihar to Mumbai in India, Jose Joseph looked around the hot, crowded compartment and wondered how to fill the time. He and his American friend Roger had twenty-six more hours to go. Joseph is the man I introduced in chapter 11, who studied traditional Indian music at a Hindu academy.

Roger pulled out his guitar and played a few English songs. The fellow passengers listened politely. Eventually they asked for Hindi songs. Roger handed the guitar to Joseph and explained that Joseph was a singer who knew Hindi music.

Joseph warned his listeners that he knew only devotional songs about Jesus. He was pretty sure every other person in the compartment was a Hindu. Someone in the crowd said, "We don't care. Just sing."

Joseph sang the first words of a bhajan: "*Yeshu naam sundaru naam.*" It means "Jesus's name is beautiful."

Several people in the train car smiled and sang back to Joseph, "*Yeshu naam sundaru naam.*"

As the song continued, more people squeezed into the compartment to see what was going on. By the end of the song, there were thirty people crammed inside. In Hindi, they were singing, "Jesus's name is beautiful; Jesus's name is sweet; Jesus's name is loving."

Joseph played song after song. The crowd, who knew the bhajan format, knew just when to sing along. When Joseph played fast songs, people danced inside the compartment and outside in the little entryway. They sang and danced for four hours. They stopped only when Joseph, exhausted, said he had to sleep.

Joseph and his friend brought worship out of the church setting and into a different place, an Indian train car. They could do this because they could embrace the whole spectrum of where the people around them were at on their journey toward Jesus. Even a crowd of Hindus who had received very little exposure to Jesus could start singing worship songs right then, right where they were.

Author Ray Oldenburg talks about social meeting venues as the "third place."[6] Most people have a home as their first place and work as a second place. If they add another gathering spot, a third place, this setting can provide some of the caring relationships they long for.

According to researcher George Barna, a lot of settings can work for spiritual third places besides church buildings. The admonition from the book of Hebrews "Let us not give up meeting together" leaves plenty of room for variety.[7] Barna writes, "The same God who is more concerned about what's in our hearts than about mindless observance of meaningless routines refuses to impose specific regulations about our religious practices."[8]

I think we're free to create a temple-like meeting space that stays open all the time. We're free to embrace the fact that many people come to faith and grow in their faith through support groups like Alcoholics Anonymous. Or we can meet as we work together to serve the community, such as picking up trash in an alley or serving meals to the hungry. We're free to meet outside, gathering where the Native Americans gathered. As Charles Eastman put it, "The murmuring trees breathe His presence; the falling waters chant His praise."[9]

According to Ray Oldenburg, the modern Western world badly needs to find these third places. In the suburbs, people increasingly isolate themselves from each other by "cocooning" and "nesting" with their big TVs and game systems. Oldenburg quotes two authors who conclude, "People are honestly trying to balance the frantic privacy of the suburbs with some kind of spontaneous public life."[10]

It's time for believers to find and create these new places, even if they find them on trains at night.

Form New Partnerships

I shoved my bag up onto an overhead rack and looked around for an open seat. I saw one and plopped down, breathing a sigh of relief. I had managed to find my way through the crowded train station in Meknes, Morocco, figure out the garbled French loudspeaker instructions, and get on the correct train.

Placing my computer bag on the floor and looking around me, I found that I was sitting beside a Moroccan man and his wife. The man wore the garb of a devout Muslim. His shirt was a cream-colored kurta that went down to his ankles, and he wore a white prayer hat. He had a thick, full beard.

To be honest, his appearance intimidated me a bit, but as he noticed my glance he smiled and introduced himself. He spoke fluent English with a French accent.

I found out he had been educated in France and now worked for the Moroccan government in Rabat. As he asked me about my family and I asked about his, I began to relax. He was a friendly, jovial man. I realized I would have the next three hours before we reached Tangier to get to know him.

For some reason, the man's kind manner helped me get over my natural reticence. I decided to find out how this devout North African Muslim perceives Christianity.

Knowing that Muslims pray by prostrating themselves at certain times during the day, I asked him how he could pray during a long journey like this if he was confined to his seat. He explained there were other ways to pray in situations like that. Then I asked, "What happens if you miss a prayer time?" I had always thought of Islam as a religion of works, and I wondered how perfect he thought he had to be to receive acceptance from God.

He stroked his beard and looked up for a moment. Then, in Arabic, he quoted a verse from the Qur'an. He translated the verse for me into English. Then he commented on it. He held his hands out before him, palms up, and moved them as though they were scales. He told me that everything is in the hands of Allah. It is completely up to His mercy whether anyone gets into paradise. He could let in someone who doesn't pray and fast and leave out someone who follows these practices diligently. We do these prayers and fasts, he said, because they are gifts from Allah to us.

I asked him many more questions about his faith, and he was always happy to answer. He would pull on his beard, recite a verse, translate it, and then give me his thoughts.

Emboldened by how well our conversation was going, I decided to ask him a riskier question. I asked, "What bothers you about Christians?"

He was reluctant to answer that one. Instead, he said something respectful about Christian people. "But surely," I said, "there are some aspects of the beliefs or the behaviors of Christians you would disagree with."

Finally, with some hesitation, he told me about the errors he saw in Christian beliefs. Christians believe in three gods, the Father, the Son, and Mary. The Christian Bible has been rewritten and corrupted. Christians believe God had sex with Mary to produce Jesus, which, he said, is a repulsive thought to a Muslim.

I asked him a few questions to clarify what he had said. Then, I asked him, "Would you like to know my perspective on those concerns?"

He said he would be happy to know my thoughts. I tried to explain the Trinity, Bible translation, and the virgin birth. As I spoke, I was painfully aware that I could not quote the Bible nearly as well as he had quoted the Qur'an. The man listened respectfully. He asked me a few questions. He seemed impressed that I had thought about these matters.

When we reached Tangier, the man and his wife said good-bye to me with great warmth. We exchanged addresses and promised to write.

I headed off to the ferry terminal with a lot of gratitude for the conversation I'd just had. I was determined to take away at least two lessons from that encounter. First, I realized that it was our devoutness that drew us together. I would have thought that the more serious a Muslim is about his faith, the more difficult it would be for me, as a Christian, to relate with him. Maybe if I had sat down beside a Muslim extremist that would have been the case. But with this man, the opposite was true. I respected him for his deep faith convictions, and he respected me for my love for God. Second, I went away determined to spend more time memorizing the Bible.

If we believe all truth is God's truth, and if we recognize that other religions can contain some truth, we can approach people of other faiths differently. We can discover that as people of faith, we have more in common than we realized. We might even see that we have more areas of agreement with some devout North Africans than we do with some secular Americans. As believers in Jesus begin to think more like this, they will discover more ways to team up with devotees of other religions and work on common concerns, like the increase of secularism.

On a grand scale, Muslims and Christians have teamed up effectively in the past. Gerald McDermott reports that in 1995, at the United Nations Conference on Population and Development in Cairo, Roman Catholics and Muslims worked together to defeat an abortion rights initiative. Had this measure passed, McDermott wrote, it would have enshrined abortion on demand as an international human right.[11]

A friend of mine in Los Angeles, Lisa Patriquin, works on forming these kinds of connections in local communities. She and the other members of the Christian-Muslim Consultative Group have created a study guide called "Standing Together."[12] This seven-week series of DVDs and guided discussions is meant to help Muslims and Christians get to know each other.

Patriquin discovered that one of the Muslims who worked with her on the curriculum attended a mosque in Newhall, a northern Los Angeles community. Since Patriquin worked for the Presbyterian denomination, she contacted the pastor of the Presbyterian church there and told him about the mosque, Unity Center of Santa Clarita. She suggested that the "Standing Together" program could help the two groups get to know each other.

Eventually members from First Presbyterian Church and Unity Center met. They were surprised to realize they worshiped in buildings that were only a block from each other. They agreed to meet regularly, using the "Standing Together" curriculum.

In the beginning they learned the meaning of religious terms, like "born again," or "*Eid.*"[13] By the end of their study, they brainstormed about possible activities or projects they might want to do together.

After hearing Lisa's story, I visited the website for Newhall Pres-
byterian Church. The site displayed typical announcements, like
"Sign up today for Lenten Study Groups." It also included an item
that showed the journey the church has been through: "Interfaith
American Red Cross blood drive, Feb. 26, 10 a.m. to 4 p.m. at the
Unity Center Mosque on 8th St."

That, I thought, is a different kind of drawing of blood between
Christians and Muslims. It's the kind of announcement I think we
will see a lot more if believers in Jesus begin to form new partnerships with the people of different faiths around them.

Pray with Your Body

In Muslim, Hindu, and Buddhist countries, I've observed people
using their bodies in worship more than I've seen in Christian traditions. When these people begin to follow Jesus, they continue to
bow, to dance, and to use other physical activities as signs of devotion—assuming they are not told to abandon these practices. What
I've seen has made me wonder at the possibilities for integrating a
person's physical being into faith. How can believers find new ways
of expressing themselves to God and new formats for gathering
together by using their bodies more in worship?

I discovered one answer in a counselor's office near Pasadena,
California. My friend Cissy Brady-Rogers, a marriage and family
therapist, leads Christ-centered yoga classes. She had invited me
to attend.

Yoga originates in Hinduism, a fact that has made some Christians reluctant to try it. Some believe the body positions themselves
have evil power. In Hinduism, the body positions, or *asanas*, of yoga
constitute one of the eight stages of yoga described in the Yoga Sutra.
Overall, the stages emphasize self-control and meditation. Hindus
consider the god Shiva to be the lord of yoga.[14] I was curious how
Brady-Rogers could turn this Hindu practice into something holy.

168

I also wondered what to wear. Would the yoga session be like a gym class, or a prayer meeting? Should I wear loose-fitting street clothes, or shorts and a T-shirt? When I arrived at Brady-Rogers's office and went into a bathroom to change, I opted for the shorts. Since it was a chilly winter day, I left my socks on.

In the yoga room, I greeted Brady-Rogers, a trim, fortyish woman whose brown hair was beginning to turn gray. She introduced me to the three other women in the room. They were all wearing color-coordinated sweat suits. They all had bare feet.

Brady-Rogers directed me to a dark blue mat. I sat and looked around. Indian-style hangings adorned the walls.

Using a remote control, Brady-Rogers turned on some quiet music. She sat on a mat in front of us, and began with a few comments.

"Today I read the parable of the soils," she said. "It reminded me of what I read somewhere recently about humility." She relayed the teaching of this author, that the root word of "humility" is "humus," which means "soil." Brady-Rogers said humility means being so low, so soiled, so aware of your earthiness that you can't be soiled any further. It gives you a freedom, she said, to follow Jesus and to obey the Spirit without being attached to how it turns out, whether you succeed or fail.

"That was really comforting to me," she said, "to think that what's important is that I'm rooted and grounded in Christ."

She then opened in prayer. "Thank you, Jesus, for your model of humility. Our desire as we do this yoga practice is to deepen our own sense of being rooted and grounded in you. May you speak to us and strengthen us as we stretch and strengthen our bodies, that our bodies would be vessels of humility for your service."

As Brady-Rogers explained how to breathe and began to tell us how to move into the various positions, I became uncomfortably aware I was the only one in the room who didn't know what I was doing.

Brady-Rogers gave me helpful tips like, "Bryan, if you take off your socks it might go better."

She also explained things I had never thought of before. When I was struggling to balance on one hand and one leg, she explained how to think about our hands.

"You'll notice there are four corners to your hands," she said. "One corner is right behind the pointer finger, one at the knuckle under the little finger, and then there are 'roots' at either corner on the outside of the wrists. Anytime you have your hands down on the ground, you want to be rooting with your full hand. You want to balance the weight evenly on your four roots, and at the same time you also want to lightly grip with your fingertips."

As the hour-long session progressed, the positions got more difficult. At one point, she said, "Okay, so come to lie on your back, leave your shoulders on the ground, draw your right knee in and lift your left leg off the ground just a little bit."

The lady next to me groaned.

I've wondered as I've traveled, could body movement play a bigger part in the gatherings of believers? Could it even define these gatherings? I think the powwow is a beautiful example of how dance can serve as the main element in a spiritual group experience. I don't see why Christ-centered powwows couldn't become one of the worship venues for Native Americans, or for people from any ethnic group who feel drawn to this format. I've also enjoyed dance as a main element in a messianic Jewish gathering. Dance could invigorate a spiritual meeting.

As Brady-Rogers led the yoga, it became clear that spirituality could also transform exercise.

Eventually she moved us into a gentle pose to help us relax. We were breathing heavily, feeling the warmth in our limbs. "If we think about our faith in Christ," Brady-Rogers observed, "a lot of what we need to be doing in our lives is rooting and hugging in, drawing in to the center of our life in Christ. The world is always pulling us out of ourselves and into a lot of craziness.

"Okay, wide legs again, same thing."

We ended with the corpse pose, which involved simply lying flat on our backs, hands at our sides, palms up. She had dimmed the light, and the music now was quiet worship music. I lay there thinking this had been like church. I thought, why couldn't this be a church?

In the book *Prayer of Heart and Body*, Thomas Ryan says he uses yoga to lead him into this kind of meditative experience. "It is less a concentration of mental faculties than a turning of one's whole being toward Another."[15]

For me, I realized the theme of grounding in Christ had hit home to me as I struggled to balance. I had tried to get the hang of the four corners of my hand as one leg was sticking out in the air behind me, my torso was turned sideways, and only one hand and one knee were on the floor. As I fought for balance, I thought of living life balanced on the gravity of my central relationship with God. This thought came from deeper within me than it would have if I had been sitting in a pew. It was a revelation that came from my body and my mind and my soul all at the same time.

Brady-Rogers told me a participant in one of her previous classes put it differently. "This was so great," the woman had told her. "It was like getting a homily and a workout all in one."

New words, new places, new partnerships, new ways of using the body—maybe that's enough for one plate. I could have gone on down the buffet line and suggested new ways to use the visual arts, inspired by Buddhist imagery or *Likay* folk dramas. I could have also envisioned a Christ-centered gathering that redeems and incorporates New Age customs and festivals.

The truth is, I can't describe what lies inside the steaming metal pans ahead of us. I don't know what dishes they hold. My purpose in writing this book wasn't to give a lot of recipes. I hope these pages provide some ingredients and some inspiration to experiment for yourself.

I realize this book probably also raises some concerns, and I'll try to answer those next.

13

What the World Needs Now

In the beginning of this book, I told you about Randy, the guy I met in Thailand back in 1998. His story about a Muslim man who followed Jesus got my mind spinning and ultimately set me on the path that led to my voyage of discovery. As I finished the research for this book, I decided to contact Randy again to get an update. I wanted to make sure I had gotten the facts of the story correct. I also wanted to find out what had happened in the decade since we first talked.

What I found out disturbed me again. Randy's story had a troubling side to it that I wasn't aware of in 1998.

In chapter 1, I told Randy's account as I first understood it. The facts are all true. They are just not complete. Now I'll tell the rest of the story.

The first man who came to Christ really did come to faith from a vision, with no contact from Christians. As he shared his faith, many others did believe, and they came to faith rapidly. In six months the circle of believers had grown to sixty-five people.

This man, though, believed he had supernatural powers. That's one of the parts I completely missed when Randy told me the story the first time. This man believed he had the divine authority to marry a woman on the spot and then sleep with her that same night. The circle of believers that grew around this man were all poor people who found hope in this man's faith and his powers. They left their jobs and moved with him to another island. A few of them sold cows to pay their way. Some of the women left their husbands behind.

Randy first met this group on the island they had moved to. He and some of his associates offered to help them. They encouraged the members of this fellowship to move back to their original community, to rejoin their families, and to go back to work. He even helped some of them earn an income with an agriculture business. He was laboring at this and bringing discipleship to the leader when the Christian organization came and took half the group to a three-month discipleship program on another island.

Randy tried to continue working with the assistant leader, who had stayed behind. That person, after getting more training, did end up continuing to lead a small group of believers in Jesus, but the group didn't really grow.

Eventually Randy and his family moved to a different location. Now they work with another Muslim ethnic group.

My journey of discovery with Randy's story mirrors the research voyage I took. In some ways, the picture became messier the closer I looked. In the beginning, these movements to get outside of the traditional culture of Christianity seemed so important, so significant, I couldn't think of anything the world needed more. During the course of my travels, though, some of my nice, neat ideas started to unravel.

For example, yes, it's exciting to think a Muslim could follow Christ and still call herself a Muslim. That would remove a lot of the Christian cultural stigma that surrounds biblical faith and would make it easier for her to eventually embrace the divinity of

Jesus. But when this woman uses the term "Muslim," even if she qualifies it to say she's a Muslim who follows Jesus, wouldn't almost anyone assume she still holds on to the main Islamic beliefs? Wouldn't a person assume she thinks the Qur'an was given by God word for word to Muhammad? Could she really believe that? Might she start questioning more and more of her previous beliefs as she studies more and more of the Bible? Might she eventually move away from the word "Muslim" as a result?

In some ways, my travels gave me more questions, not fewer. As I met more and more people who were pursuing biblical faith outside the Western box, I wondered how to put it all into balance. What beliefs do I agree with and which ones don't I agree with? How can these new forms of faith in Christ coexist with traditional Christianity? Where does this cultural trend fit within the overall purposes of God for the world?

I found that I was developing three main convictions about how to put this new development into perspective. I'll explain each of them in this chapter:

- Maintain a high regard for Christianity, even in its Western format.
- Experiment courageously.
- Use many forms of incarnational witness.

And at the end of my journey, I realized I'd discovered something the world needs more than a diverse Christ-following culture.

Maintain a High Regard for Western Christianity

In this book, I've described the stifling effects of the spread of a franchised Western version of faith in Jesus. I've argued that the label "Christian" isn't biblically necessary. I have also put forward the views of those who say that many of the cherished trappings of Christian faith come primarily from tradition and not from the

Bible. They say practices like meeting in a church building, listening to a Sunday sermon, or forming choirs aren't necessary to follow the teaching of Scripture. Those who don't find life in these kinds of activities are free to find other ways to meet together and grow in their faith.

In saying all this, I don't want to belittle Christianity. For many, including me, the historic creeds and formats of Christian culture provide a good way to worship God and walk in God's ways. I don't see that changing, even if the introduction of foreign flavors gradually changes the tastes of believers in the Western world.

In my opinion, for all their faults, Christians have provided the world with far more good than bad. Historical and statistical analysis supports that view. For the Project on Religion and Economic Change, professor Robert Woodberry of the University of Texas carefully studied Protestant and Catholic missionary activity from the beginning of the nineteenth century until the middle of the twentieth century.[1] While he admitted most missionaries carried with them an attitude of cultural superiority, he said the criticisms of mission as imperialistic are exaggerated and not based on historical fact.

Often, missionaries had a higher view of indigenous peoples than the contemporaries of their day, Woodberry claimed. As an example, he cited James Hunt, the man who created the term "anthropology." Hunt criticized Christians for their educational programs and "argued that dark skinned people were a different species, mentally inferior to whites, and could not be 'civilized' through education."[2]

The emphasis of Christian missionaries on educating everyone, even women and the poor, and promoting literacy for all, is still measurable, Woodberry found. These efforts still benefit billions of people "in the educational enrollments, infant mortalities, and levels of political democracy in societies around the world."[3]

It's a legacy that every member of the body of Christ can cherish, whether the member of that body goes to Sunday school every week, like I do, or whether he attends a jamaat on Fridays.

We can even cherish Christianity's Western culture. In a global-ized world, it's the very westernness of Christianity that appeals to huge segments of people in many countries. I saw that fact clearly on my first trip to India. I went to visit a friend in Hyderabad and felt as though I was entering a new world. I had just come from a mostly Hindu city in the north. There, I had watched gaunt holy men dressed in orange walking by me on the road. Most of the Indian Christ-followers I interviewed carefully used Hindu-friendly language. When they met, they took their sandals off and sat on the floor around incense and marigolds.

Then I left this community, flew to Hyderabad, and visited a friend's church on Sunday. We pulled up outside a large building surrounded with white tents filled with plastic chairs. My friend's boyfriend parked in a lot crammed with row after row of scooters. Inside, the place was packed. We spotted three free chairs near the back and headed toward them. This was the second of the three Sunday services.

According to my friend, this church, New Life Assembly of God, was the second largest church in Hyderabad. She said the largest church incorporates traditional Indian culture. Everyone takes off their shoes, leaves them outside the sanctuary, and sits on the floor, men on one side and women on the other. The services can last five hours.

New Life Assembly of God was not like that. As we squeezed down the row to our seats, the worship team had already begun their first song, "Blessed Be Your Name," a song I knew from my own church in Colorado. In fact, as I turned and looked at the worship team, I thought this whole church looked as if it had been lifted up from Colorado, flown across the ocean, and plopped down here in Hyderabad. There were about the same number of singers up on stage as I would have seen at my church, three ladies and two men. Some of them raised their hands, as did some of the people in the crowd. An enormous screen filled the wall behind the band with a scene of clouds and sky. I saw a woman and a man operating cameras for the video overflow tents around the building.

All the songs we sang I knew well. In fact, at one point the worship pastor mentioned he had just come back from a trip to Chicago and Maui and he had learned a song that he had brought back with him.

Although the congregation around me contained people of all ages, most looked to be in their twenties and thirties. The young couple in front of me fit that description. The man was nicely dressed in a crisp blue shirt and khakis. His wife wore a wine-colored sari. During one song, I watched the man slowly shake his head, evidently moved by the words.

After the service, groups of congregants stood around outside in the tents. Some ate pastries filled with potato, like small Samosas. I watched a boy run up to his parents wearing a paper crown he had colored purple. Most of the people I passed seemed to be speaking Telegu or some other Indian language. The service, though, had been conducted entirely in English.

I wondered at the stories each of these men and women could tell. My friend said most of the people she knew in the church came from Hindu backgrounds. Obviously the Americanness of the church didn't put them off. Thousands of Indians in this predominantly Hindu and Muslim city had found this church a place they could call home. I guessed that the electric guitars and the drum set, the slick visuals on the stage, and even the English language all played a part in drawing them here.

"And why not?" I thought. On the C-Scale (p. 31), this would be a C1 church. It was almost as Western as it could get. I asked myself, how can I do anything but praise God for how this church has touched the lives of all these people? Why would I want to make them all sit on the floor around candles?

There's a term for that method. It's called "salvage anthropology." This term describes efforts to force traditional practices on people who no longer want them. According to professor Charles

Kraft, many cultures contain groups of people who want to become modern, which often means adopting more Western customs.

Yet Kraft warns against assuming a whole nation wants to modernize just because there are large groups who adopt the latest European fad. Many others, in the same society, hang on to traditions.

He speculates about South Korea as an example. According to *Operation World*, the growth of Christianity in Korea has "all but stopped," stuck for years at roughly 25 to 30 percent.[4] Professor Kraft wonders if the predominantly Western character of Christianity in Korea has contributed to this situation. "Could it be," he asks, "that it will take a more traditional approach to Christianity to attract the other three-quarters of the population?"[5]

I think it's good for most societies to have fellowships of believers in Christ all across the C-Scale, from very Western all the way to very ethnic. In most countries, though, the problem hasn't been providing the Western options. There are many of those. It's the other side of the spectrum that has been missing. There hasn't been any option for those who want to worship in a way that reflects their own culture. That's the reason I think the time is right to explore highly traditional options, while still affirming the value of Western forms of faith.

I left Hyderabad impressed by what I'd seen. In one part of the city, a lot of people could meet together for worship, sitting on the floor, in bare feet. Another group only a few miles away could stand to sing a worship song imported the week before from Hawaii. I think it's good to make room for both.

Experiment Courageously

As I've traveled through Asia, Europe, Africa, the Middle East, and the Americas, I've met people with widely different views on the idea of following Jesus outside of traditional Christian culture.

I've visited people with extreme perspectives both in favor of this approach and against it.

In a hotel room in a large city in South Asia, I watched as a man demonstrated how he does his daily liturgical prayers. He was wearing a long, olive-green kurta with the baggy pants underneath called pajamas. The outfit was beautifully tailored. He had brown hair and wore a closely-trimmed moustache with a long beard. Taking off his sandals, he stood next to my bed and showed me how he bowed down to the floor in stages.

This man, Ahmed, had taken an Arabic name used by both Muslims and Christians in this country. He had grown up in California, where he played in a Christian punk band. He told me he never really identified with Christian culture, hadn't labeled himself as a Christian, and the rock music was a way to express himself in another way.

Then, in South Asia, he met friends who followed Jesus in the Muslim context. He admired the biblical traditions in their culture, something he found lacking in his own. After years of prayer, research, and considering the earliest references of church history, he and his family incorporated some of these traditions into their lives, faith, and outward practice. He gave me Scripture references for his use of bowing, lifting hands in prayer, and wearing robe-like clothing.[6] Ahmed still continually evaluates the practices he uses.

He said his outer dress now reflects his real identity inside. He doesn't give himself a label, but doesn't object when Muslims assume that he is one of them. He communicates that he is a follower and servant of Jesus.

I met Ahmed on the evening before the first day of Ramadan. Over the next thirty days, he planned to meet with a few Muslims who had either decided to follow Jesus or were exploring the person of Christ. They would meet in the evenings after breaking their fast, and they planned to read through the entire New Testament together.

A constant theme for Ahmed and the Sufi Muslim friends he meets in the community is "*Wa Qurabbi Zidnii Ilm'a*," which means, "O Lord, advance me in your knowledge." They continue to gather, reading the Word of God, praying, and sharing meals together.

I can imagine that some critics of the movements I studied might watch Ahmed's daily prayers and might claim that Ahmed was a Christian and then became a Muslim in order to reach Muslims. I don't think Ahmed would agree with any of that.

If that accusation was true, though, most of the supporters of these movements would not be able to endorse Ahmed's approach. Personally, I would find it deceptive.

I think the reality of Ahmed's story, though, showed me that in an individual's sincere search for how to follow God, there's more room for experimentation than I realize.

On the other extreme, I met with another man in the corner of a large meeting room at a hotel in Thailand. It was evening, and as we talked, the staff around us were busy bundling up tablecloths and turning off lights, getting the room ready for another day. The man I was talking to, Georges Houssney, grew up in Lebanon in an Orthodox family. In his early teens, he decided to follow Christ. He had such a fervent faith that he went door-to-door telling people about Jesus. By the age of eighteen, he had started five churches.

After college, Houssney got involved in a project to translate the Bible in a way that would make it more accessible to Muslims. The translators wanted to substitute a term that means "beloved of God" for the term "Son of God," a name for Jesus that Muslims often misunderstand and find offensive. Houssney field-tested the new term, and he said that Muslims found it confusing. So he opposed the use of the term and eventually prevailed. He has continued to argue against what he sees as excesses in Christian efforts to make the gospel relevant to other cultures.

In one article he wrote, Houssney called the term "Muslim follower of Jesus" naive. He said, "The truth is that as soon as you mention Christ in context of the Bible, you are tagged as a Christian whether you like it or not."[7] He admitted that Muslims have misperceptions about Christianity, but he said the answer is to clarify the meaning of the word "Christian," not to abandon it.

In my conversation with Houssney, he told me in his experience, most Muslims who come to Christ want to leave Islam, not stay in it.

Before I met Houssney, I might have assumed he was against every practice used by the movements I studied. That wasn't true, though. He told me he uses one of those approaches, the use of the Qur'an to point to the Bible.

The debate between people like Houssney and people like Ahmed used to take place only in remote meeting rooms like that hotel in Thailand. Now, though, the discussion has increasingly entered more public spaces, like college lecture halls, church auditoriums, and even the pages of magazines like *Christianity Today*.[8]

As the discussion has gotten wider, the Christ-centered communities labeled C5 on the C-Scale, those in which people still call themselves Hindus, Muslims, or Buddhists, have received a lot of thoughtful criticism. As I visited some of those fellowships, and as I spent time with some of those critics, I've had to rethink my own position on C5 many times.

Two of the criticisms weigh heaviest on me: is it deceptive, and is it syncretism?

The charge of syncretism means that believers in Jesus mix together teachings from the Bible and beliefs from another religion to create a new blend. The people who defend C5 respond to this charge in two ways.

Some say, yes, C5 believers have syncretism in their views, and so do American Christians and Dutch Christians and Brazilian Christians. According to professor Charles Kraft, "Wherever there are imperfect understandings made by imperfect people, there will be syncretism." He said there's no way to stamp out all syncretism, whether it exists in a materialistic Western church or a legalistic non-Western one. Instead, he wrote, "Helping people to move from where they are to more ideal expressions of Christian faith is what we need to address ourselves to." Kraft advises both national leaders and missionaries to "stop fearing syncretism."[9]

Others respond to the charge of syncretism by addressing the underlying question: Do these Muslim or Hindu followers of Jesus believe the foundational teachings of the Bible or don't they? When I've asked this question, most people say, "Yes, they do." I've been surprised how few times I've heard about strange beliefs like the ones Randy told me about.

In one study, Fuller Seminary, PEW Research, and Global Partners for Development teamed up to survey 4,500 mostly C5 believers in a Muslim part of South Asia. They interviewed 72 leaders of this movement and found that 97 percent said "Jesus is the only Savior." The same percentage made it clear that "they are not saved because of Muhammad's prayers." An equally high number, 96 percent, still viewed the Qur'an as one of the holy books. More than half, but only slightly more than half, could affirm that "Allah is Father, Son and Holy Spirit."[10]

As one who participated in this research back in 1998 and has followed this group regularly ever since, Dudley Woodberry, dean emeritus at Fuller Seminary, reports that his interviews of members of the group have led him to conclude they show the evidence of the leading of the Holy Spirit, "they are highly dependent on the Bible," and that as time goes on, both the Bible and other disciples of Jesus "become increasingly important in their spiritual growth." Taken as individuals, Woodberry wrote, "Many of these . . . have manifested the indwelling of the Spirit of God by their spiritual fruit, wisdom, and devotion."[11]

In my own journey, I've found it easier to put to rest the concerns about syncretism than I have the other major criticism I heard, that this approach is deceptive. One of the thoughtful critics of the movements I studied is Gary Corwin, associate editor of *Evangelical Missions Quarterly*. He wonders how a person can utter the Muslim confession or bow in the salat prayers without communicating "adherence to the doctrines of Islam." A Muslim follower of Jesus can explain their actions away through "theological gymnastics" or appealing to multiple meanings of words, Corwin continued, but, "It is hard to imagine, however, that they will not ultimately be viewed as deceit. In light of the centuries-old accusation by Muslims that Christians are deceivers, at best it has to be considered a highly questionable strategy."[12]

One of the areas of debate has focused on whether C5 should be seen as a temporary state or a permanent one. In other words, for a man who calls himself a Muslim who follows Jesus, would his grandchildren still use that way of describing themselves? Or would they eventually come to see the similarities between themselves and Christians and start to see themselves more as part of the global body of Christ? Would they perhaps drift between C3 where they would accept the term "Christian," and C4 where they would use something unique to call themselves, and C5 where they would still identify with the culture of their heritage? That flexibility describes the actual practice of many believers I met in Bangladesh, a picture I was happy to see.

When I began my journey, I saw good reasons for the permanence of C5. Now, though, while I can see that in some cultural settings a C5 identity could work for generations, I think in many others it will end up having a more transitional, or at least fluid, role. The issue that has changed my view is this issue of deception.

A follow-up question then could be, if C5 isn't acceptable two generations down the road, why would it ever be acceptable? If it's deceptive, isn't it deceptive right from the beginning? Based on the people I met and the groups of believers I visited, I would say, no, it's not necessarily deceptive from the beginning.

I have met Muslims who sincerely see themselves as having come to faith in Jesus through the teaching of the Qur'an, a revelation that was given to the world through Muhammad. They sincerely believe that the word "Muslim" describes their identity and convictions.

Similarly, I have met Hindus who follow Sadguru Yeshu and I've asked them, "Aren't you actually Christians by another name?" While they recognize the similarities in belief, in terms of cultural practices they see themselves as very different. They bring their Hindu culture of music, the format of meeting, the festivals, and the rituals into their bhakti-style, single-minded devotion to Jesus. For them, it's a Hindu faith in Jesus, not a Christian one.

I have a hard time saying the same thing about the Buddhist world. With its lack of belief in a creator God, I could only imagine the use of the term "Buddhist" in a cultural sense. For example, "I come from a Buddhist background and I call myself a Child of God." That's a C4 statement, not a C5 one.

That's my own comfort zone at the moment, and I'm reluctant to promote it to others. Part of the reason is because of people like Ahmed, whose individual stories break the mold of my neat categories. Part of the reason is because so much of this is still in the process of being figured out. As Charles Kraft says, "Each attempt to construct a localized, 'ethnic' theology must still be seen as experimental."[13]

Another part of the reason is because of how much damage has been done by people who have said "this far and no farther."

One Christmas, I went to visit my father and mother in Vancouver, Canada. On the coffee table, I noticed an old, leather-bound book I had never seen before. I opened the metal clasp and flipped through the pages. It was a Dutch Bible. I was intrigued to see printed music in the back, where maps and a concordance would normally be. Many of the songs seemed to have the word "Psalms" printed above them.

I asked my father about this. He said the Bible had belonged to my grandmother. In the back it had the 150 Psalms put to music. It also contained 29 hymns. My father said the hymns were a later addition. Due to the fact that some of the hymns put Christian words to popular tunes, it was not easy for some Dutch believers to accept them in the beginning. My father told me that when he came to Canada in 1949, if a hymn was played in the church he left in the Netherlands, there were still people who would have felt so offended they would have gotten up and walked out.

It's hard to imagine now that hymns were ever so controversial. If the people who stormed out of church at the singing of a hymn had been granted their wish, all we would have to sing today would be 150 songs, one for each Psalm.

If constructing ethnic theology is experimental, I think it's time to experiment courageously. It's time to experiment on behalf of the huge number of Muslims, Hindus, Buddhists, and tribal people who face cultural barriers between themselves and faith in Jesus. It's also time to experiment for the sake of the increasing number of young people in the West who are leaving the Christian church behind.

Use Many Forms of Incarnational Witness

I have some friends who have lived in a Muslim country for more than two decades. During that time, they have lived through two wars. Once, they and their little children huddled with their Muslim friends in a downstairs room as mortar rounds fell in the city near them. During their time in this country, they have brought electricity for the first time to numerous villages by organizing community cooperatives. They have arranged medical care for people in need. They have researched more productive methods for planting wheat. They have played games with orphans. They have prayed for people in Jesus's name, like a twelve-year-old who was traumatized by a rocket landing in the yard when she was two.

I know this family treats Muslims and their faith with respect, but I don't know where they stand on the C-Scale. There is something in their life that speaks louder to me, so I haven't even thought to ask them their views on the scale.

When I think of this family, I think of my visit to a poor neighborhood in a city in Bangladesh. In this community the main industry is street sweeping. Those who clean the streets bring home refuse to sort and sell. As I walked around, I saw piles of paper, and a whole room full of the worn foam bottoms of flip-flops. The tiny cinder-block dwellings had narrow walkways between them that occasionally opened up to small common areas where women stood with buckets by hand pumps. Most of the people in this community could not read or write. They all followed the teachings of the Muslim faith.

I squatted down in a small cement room and watched a young man laugh with two children. The man, dressed in a kurta and jeans, sat cross-legged on a mat next to a metal trunk and a simple bamboo shelf. The shelf held a few brightly colored boxes of medicine.

The man was part of a team of six, one from South Korea and the rest from Bangladesh, who come daily to this community to do medical work. They offer simple remedies, like oral rehydration therapy for diarrhea. Sometimes the sick visit them in this little room. More often, though, the members of this team go to the bedridden in their homes.

Many times the team members realize that the treatments they have to offer are insufficient to cure a person's illness. They ask if they can pray with this person, and when they pray, they pray in the name of Isa al-Masih.

The members of this team all come from Christian backgrounds, but they use Muslim-friendly language to talk about faith. This at first confused members of the community, who couldn't tell if these people were Christians or Muslims. Eventually enough people showed interest in Isa that the team started a small fellowship group that meets once a week.

At this meeting, men and women sit separately from each other. They place the Bible on a stand, like the one used for the Qur'an. The meeting starts with a story told from the Bible. The group might ask questions or discuss it. Then the leader of the meeting asks for prayer requests and they close in prayer. When I visited, between thirty and fifty people attended this meeting.

The health-care team offers medical assistance to everyone regardless of their interest in Isa. They also provide child care during the day for families when both parents have to work. They have served the community for more than ten years.

I asked the leader of the team about her goals in this community. She said, "We're just trying to demonstrate who God is. Our particular way of doing that is through health care."

I think that's what the world needs most. It needs Christ-followers to go out there, like this team has done, and love people in Jesus's name. The majority of the world's population has not had the opportunity to meet people who live out their biblical faith among them. According to research done by the Center for the Study of Global Christianity, more than eight of every ten Muslims, Hindus, and Buddhists do not personally know any Christians.[14]

There's a danger that a focus on cultural diversity can lead to a perspective that all we need to do is get our strategy right. I think Mahatma Gandhi's advice for Christians provides a good framework for avoiding that mind-set.

"I would suggest four things," Gandhi told his friend E. Stanley Jones.

"First . . . that all of your Christians, missionaries and all, must begin to live more like Jesus Christ.

"Second . . . that you practice your religion without adulterating it, or toning it down.

"Third . . . that you emphasize love and make it your working force, for love is central in Christianity.

"Fourth . . . that you study the non-Christian religions more sympathetically to find the good in them, to have a more sympathetic approach to people."[15]

I think the greatest need in the world, the absolute top need, is for more people to go out into every community and live like that.

14

Revolution in Chicago

I thought my journey was finished. I was back home, busy sorting through pages of transcripts. During my many voyages, I had seen everything I'd hoped to see, and more. I thought it was time to pull it all together.

But then I had lunch with Kristin.

We met at a Middle Eastern restaurant in Colorado Springs. Kristin was wearing an orange and green Rasta hat. Her pretty, earnest face gazed at me from across the table as she told me about her latest adventures. After finishing her studies in elementary education in Chicago, she had gotten a job in Jerusalem as a student teacher. After a year there and several months of training with a mission agency, she spent the summer with a couple of friends in southern India. They set up a coffee shop at a village along the hippie trail.

Now, she had come back to Chicago for a while, volunteering with her fiancé at a place called the South Asian Friendship Center. She had left Chicago briefly for this visit to Colorado.

She asked me about my own journeys. I told her some of the highlights.

She said, "Dude, you've got to come to Chicago!" After all the places I'd been, she insisted, I had to see everything happening in one city. She talked about Hindus she knew who followed Jesus, about young friends of hers who were living out their faith in non-traditional ways. She said I could see how this whole trend might play out in a Western, multiethnic city. The future, she said, was right there, right where she lived in Chicago. She urged me to come at least for a few days.

I told her I'd think about it.

A couple of weeks later, I decided to go.

The Satsang

The morning after I arrived in Chicago, I walked along Devon Street and looked for the South Asian Friendship Center. I passed shops like Gandhi Electronics, Sari Sapne, and Shah Jehel Grocery. Then I turned a corner, and there it was. A sign on the window said "Free English Class."

Inside, a mat held two pairs of shoes. I took mine off as well. I could smell incense. Ahead of me were bookshelves, a counter with a big thermos of chai, and three clocks with the time for Chicago, Karachi, and Mumbai. The lobby area opened into a room full of cushions and carpets.

A man responded to the jingling of the door and came out of the room to greet me. He was an Indian man with a short beard. He was wearing a long, yellow-orange kurta and brown dress pants. He smiled and shook my hand and invited me to get a cup of chai.

I held the hot, milky drink in a Styrofoam cup and found a place to sit in the room. The man I met, Anil Yesudas, busied himself arranging pillows and distributing cream-colored booklets around the room. I picked up a booklet and thumbed through it. On the cover, under Hindi script, were the words "Christocentric Satsang."

Three women arrived and took their seats. Yesudas found a place on the floor. He sat cross-legged before an incense stick burning in a holder, a silver plate with a cross on it, a conch shell, and a book on a stand. He placed an orange cloth over his lap. He asked if any of the ladies had a song suggestion.

One woman recommended a bhajan called "God, We Worship You," and led out in it. All the others joined her. Yesudas played along on a small gong. One of the ladies picked up a tambourine and accompanied him. As the group sang more songs, other people trickled in. Six more ladies found places to sit. Two men followed them, one of whom sat next to Yesudas.

Once everyone had arrived, Yesudas directed the group to chant several of the mantras from the cream-colored booklet. They chanted the verses from Colossians 1:15–20. Another mantra proclaimed the names of Jesus, whom Yesudas called "Lord Sri Jesus Christ." When applied to a deity, the word *Sri* means "holy." As the group declared Hindi names that meant "Word of God," "Glory of God," "Alpha and Omega," and many others, Yesudas rang a bell in time with the rhythmic, singsong words.

The bell resounded sharply. The chanting and bell ringing sounded exactly like a Hindu ceremony I witnessed once at a temple in Bali, Indonesia.

Then the man next to Yesudas began to speak. He was also an Indian man, wearing a beige sweater. I found out later that this man's name is Vinod Isaac. "The Lord Jesus Christ often talked about faith," Isaac said. "Today we will look at a story that tells us how faith works."

With an open Bible on a stand in front of him, Isaac told about the woman who touched Jesus in the hope that she would be healed from her bleeding. As he relayed the events of the story, Isaac would say a few sentences in Hindi and then translate them into English.

At the end of the story, Isaac concluded, "The Lord Jesus Christ asks one more question, 'When the Son of Man comes back, will He find faith?'" Isaac explained how Jesus offers forgiveness. "So let the Lord Jesus Christ help us today," Isaac said, "that our sins may be forgiven and that we may have faith."

Yesudas then led a time of silence. Afterward they passed around a basket with cards that had Bible verses written in Hindi and English. Yesudas began another chant, with hands pressed in front of him, rocking slightly back and forth. He blew the conch shell three times. He explained the shell symbolizes the trumpet call of God, that the Lord Jesus Christ will come back.

He invited the group to share prayer requests. One lady mentioned her uncle in India who was suffering with kidney stones. One of the ladies in the group prayed for this man. Then after another song, a ringing of the bell, and a final chant, Yesudas said, "May the grace of the Lord Sri Jesus Christ be with you."

With that, some members of the group stood up to get more chai. As the people talked and walked out, I had a chance to visit with Yesudas.

I found out Yesudas grew up in a Christian home in North India. His father, George David, was a pastor, as was his grandfather. As a young man, Yesudas grew his beard long and dreamed of becoming a missionary holy man like Sadhu Sundar Singh. He wanted to sit in Hindu temples and make friends there. His father, though, convinced Yesudas that he could make a greater long-term impact by getting a job and having a family. Much of what Yesudas practices he attributes to the inspiration of his father.

Yesudas studied to become a pharmacist and got an MBA as well. He came to the United States after his parents arranged a marriage for him with an Indian woman who lived in the States. In Chicago he earned two graduate degrees, in health law and community development. Then he got a job with a pharmaceutical company in Michigan.

While there, he spent a lot of time in Hindu temples. He went to the temple before or after work from Monday through Friday. He sat there in the temple and he asked, "Lord, what should I do?" He watched and listened. He got to know the people and began to understand their perspective. He developed his ideas for the satsang in that temple.

Now, he said the satsang format has become a regular part of his own faith in Christ. He hopes it provides an environment that feels familiar to Hindus.

Yesudas told me a few of the people I saw in the room during the satsang were Hindus. The man who frequently plays the tabla drum works at the local Hindu temple.

Yesudas started the satsang in a Hindu temple in Michigan in 2004, continued it there for five years, and then moved it to the South Asian Friendship Center after he left his pharmaceutical job and moved back to Chicago. Now he occasionally teaches two graduate classes at Moody, one of them on Hinduism. His business card says he is an "interfaith activist and housing rights activist."

Many people don't know what to call him. If someone asks if he is a Christian, he will reply, "Yes, I am a follower of the Lord Jesus." He wants to put the emphasis on devotion to Jesus, and not on "participation in a Western sect." One Nepali lady who came to the satsang asked Yesudas, "Are you a Hindu?" He replied, "I am a follower of the Lord Jesus." "But you must be a Hindu," she said. Yesudas resists labeling himself.

If other Hindus want to give the believers the Hindu label, as the Nepali woman did to him, Yesudas said it's okay. "If the Hindu gives the name, then another Hindu will respect it."

He doesn't have much hope that a Western form of Christianity will ever reach the Hindu world. He wants to see a satsang movement catch fire and grow in parallel to Western denominations. Even in Hindu neighborhoods in Chicago, like the one around us near Devon Street, Yesudas would like to see Jesus temples proliferating. He would like to see buildings that are devoted to Jesus open twenty-four hours a day, with no memberships required.

He said faith in Christ needs to be practiced in multicultural ways. It's not about trying to decrease resistance of the Hindus to the biblical message, he insisted. "Our intention is to make the biblical message clear."

Erika's Neighbors

I had to leave the South Asian Friendship Center to meet Kristin for lunch. As I walked along, I imagined Jesus temples in the midst of the homes and businesses around me. When I neared Kristin's apartment, I passed a mosque. Many Muslim immigrants live in this part of town.

Kristin was staying with a young married couple. She introduced me to Erika, who was pregnant and approaching the baby's due date in a few weeks. I sat in the sunlight filtering through curtains made of orange Indian fabric, held a cup of tea, and chatted with Erika.

She told me she used to teach a knitting class at a refugee center. Many of the women who came to the class were from Iraq. She met a single mother with four young children. "Our talks were immediately deep," Erika said. "She was seeking guidance from God. She wanted to draw near God, but she felt lost."

Erika and her husband got to know this woman and the woman's sister, who lived in their neighborhood. They had become such close friends that Erika and her husband had gone on a camping trip with them on the weekend before I arrived.

In the beginning, as a way to encourage her friend, Erika told her stories from the Bible, like the story of the prodigal son. Erika prayed with her for peace, for guidance, for hope. Eventually Erika's friend and her sister started attending an evening dinner and Bible study hosted by some friends of Erika and her husband.

"She had quite a few dreams given her by God," Erika said. In one dream, Jesus came and gave the woman flowers.

At the time, Erika was at Moody Theological Seminary taking intercultural studies. She told her friend she was studying the Bible, and her friend said she had a great respect for that. "I love Jesus," the woman said.

Erika said her friend also loves being Muslim. Her friend now has heard both what Jesus says about Himself and what her Muslim upbringing has taught her about Jesus not being God. Erika said as much as she wants her friend to have a mature understanding of what the Bible teaches, she knows everyone learns in steps.

She's not sure, though, if she wants her friend eventually to call herself a Christian. "What's in a name?" Erika asked. "It's the relationship that's important."

In their neighborhood, Erika and her husband have brought bread to Iraqis, have played pool in an Indian family's basement, have helped neighbors with computer issues, and have received parenting advice. I could tell that Erika cares for her friends in many ways she didn't mention. While we were talking, she was interrupted by a phone call. "Oh, hi, Amira," Erika said. "You have to take the car to the shop? I'll meet you at 3:15. That would be perfect."

I asked Erika what she's learned from all the friendships she's made. After a long pause, she said, "It's just such a privilege to see the greatness of the mercy and love of God, to see that played out in someone's life. It's a reminder of why Jesus needs to be shared. Look at what He does! Why wouldn't you want this for people? With this particular friend, I saw how tender and gentle Jesus was. For me, that grew my love for Him, to see Him so sweetly and gently loving my friend."

Jesus People USA

The next morning, Kristin and I, without an appointment, headed over to the headquarters of Jesus People USA. We entered a tall building. The sign on the awning outside read "Friendly Towers."

Inside, I saw two young ladies who were folding clothes at a table and I tried to explain our purpose in coming. One of the women directed us to an office to our left. They told us to ask for Robert. When we came to the office door, Robert Goodwin got up from his laptop and greeted us. Goodwin, who looked to be in his forties, had sleeve tattoos, colorful images that covered both arms. He said he would talk with us, but first he wanted to check with another person. He pulled out an iPhone and talked to someone named Jon. After the call, he smiled and said Jon Trott could make time for us. Goodwin said Trott was the perfect guy for us to talk to. He drew a little map to help us find the building where Trott was working.

Kristin and I left the Friendly Towers, which apparently provided housing for elderly people who couldn't afford other care, and walked to a smaller building, which was a shelter for women. Inside, a young lady at a small wooden desk asked us to wait while she told Jon we had arrived. The lady's face bristled with piercings—around each ear, and on her eyebrows, nose, and lips.

Trott, a tall man with gray, spiky hair, greeted us warmly and looked for a place for us to meet. We chose a small kitchen and sat on metal chairs by an old Formica table. He told us, as far as he knew, Jesus People USA is one of the last remaining Jesus People communes. The four hundred members of the community share their lives, run a large roofing company, and use the proceeds to support themselves and their ministries, like the shelter for women.

When Trott was a young man, this model of Christian community appealed to him. He became a Christian in Montana through the witness of hippie-style people. It wasn't until he went to a Christian university that he encountered the evangelical culture. He found the experience disorienting. "There was a look you were supposed to have," he recalled. "There was a lingo you were supposed to have."

He felt like an outsider. Eventually Trott dropped out and joined Jesus People USA. He had heard about the group through their magazine, *Cornerstone*. He came because he didn't want the normal

Christian subculture. He wanted to become a disciple of Jesus. He wanted something different.

Just as Trott was saying this, the door to the kitchen opened, and a middle-aged man poked his face in, looked at me, and said, "Somebody told me you're a professional electrician."

I said, "Sorry, I think that's a different guy." He apologized and closed the door.

Still today, Jesus People USA attracts people like Trott, people who didn't find what they were looking for in traditional churches and hope they can find it in this place. One such group Trott called the "travelers." He said a number of kids are hopping trains and traveling across the country, like the hobos used to do. Some of these travelers have found their way into a ten-month discipleship program at Jesus People USA.

One traveler had been in and out of drug use, sexually involved with one girlfriend after another, married, and divorced. He came from a Catholic background. "It was never that he dissed God exactly," Trott explained, "but God wasn't really in the mix." This young man encountered the gospel, believed, and then started using drugs again. He eventually arrived in Chicago at Jesus People USA and joined the discipleship program. Now he helps lead the program, assisting other young people as they go through similar transitions.

Most of these people wouldn't darken the door of a suburban church, but they have found a safe haven at this commune. Trott, though, has no illusions that the members of Jesus People USA have somehow broken free of Christian subculture. They've just created their own subculture.

The members of Jesus People USA noticed this fact, Trott said, one Sunday in the late '70s or early '80s. They were all sitting in church in their hippy finest. The girls wore long jean skirts. The guys had beards, long hair, and flannel shirts. "We were the quintessential hippies," Trott said. "We were better hippies than the hippies were hippies."

Then a girl walked in sporting a five-inch red mohawk. She was the singer for a Christian band. "It was like a discordant note played on a piano," Trott recalled. "There was a moment of confusion. We had to go, 'Okay, we're not on the cultural cutting edge anymore.'" It was a watershed moment, Trott said. Would they embrace this or be repelled by it?

The problem of homogeneity was one they faced and one Trott said the evangelical church as a whole faces. How do we get beyond it?

Trott suggested becoming more biblically literate, not just proof texting through verses but actually reading the whole book. Also he talked about how the tight relationship between evangelicals and one kind of politics turns off many young people.

He was reluctant to offer Jesus People USA as a model to follow, but he was willing to offer inspiration. "Maybe we are a hope for the church," he said. "If we can do something this crazy, you could do something less crazy."

He would like to urge people to find ways to invite others into a humble journey of following Jesus. "Do something less radical," he insisted, "but do something. Create devices, create structures, create possibilities."

The Temple

"Do you know the way to the Hare Krishna temple?" Kristin asked a man who was walking his dog. Kristin and I had decided to end my time in Chicago with visits to two of the places people I met had referred to, the Hare Krishna temple and a mosque. We were now a little lost.

Kristin had mentioned the Hare Krishna temple when she told me about her tutoring work at the South Asian Friendship Center. She taught a boy and a girl from a family who had moved here from India just four months earlier. After two months of attending the satsang, the boy had learned to play the tabla and would close his eyes and sing the worship songs to Jesus. He said he wanted to pray to commit his life to Christ. But his mother asked Anil Yesudas, "Can he do all this while he worships other gods?"

Yesudas explained the seriousness of this step. He gave the boy a New Testament to read.

The boy had posted a picture of Jesus in the house. But Kristin told me he also said, "I went to the Hare Krishna temple and I danced like anything."

Ahead, Kristin and I finally saw a three-story brick building with a small yellow sign in the front, International Society for Krishna Consciousness. We went in, took off our shoes, and spent a short time in the main room sitting on mats.

As we prepared to leave, a woman asked us if we had any questions. We inquired about some of the statues we had seen. The woman then asked us about ourselves.

Kristin told her about the satsang on Thursdays. The woman seemed intrigued, so Kristin invited her to come. Kristin told her she'd been learning to chant. I had been there when Yesudas worked with Kristin in one of these sessions.

The woman seemed genuinely interested. She asked Kristin what kind of chants she'd been learning. Kristin paused for a moment to refresh her mind. She explained, "This chant means we worship you, Father, Spirit, Jesus." Then she closed her eyes and sang these words: "*Santanan shri pita, putra, pavitratmane namaha.*"

The woman seemed pleased with the chant and went to get us a booklet, which she gave me as we left. The booklet referred to Krishna as the "reservoir of pleasure." The woman said, "You can pray to God to help you. The purpose of all religions is to connect you to God."

As we walked away, Kristin told me more about her own journey. From an early age, Kristin felt a curiosity about nontraditional forms of faith in Jesus. When she was fourteen, she met some Messianic Jews in Colorado. She started attending their Saturday service. While at Moody, she learned about Islamic culture. During Ramadan she would fast at lunchtime and pray each day for the Muslim world. In Chicago she volunteered in ministries to the Jewish community and with Emmaus, an organization that works with male prostitutes. She also got involved with the 24/7 prayer movement.

She told me when she was teaching in Jerusalem, she would sometimes get fed up with the constant focus on Israel. So she would go into her room, shut the door, light incense, put on some Aradhna Indian–style music, and meditate on Jesus. When she was in India setting up the coffee shop, she worked with an Indian pastor who wanted to learn more about Jewish customs. So she organized a Jewish Shabbat meal for the Indian congregation.

The eclectic nature of her spiritual interests fascinated me, but frustrated many of her friends. "Usually the people I meet stick to one thing," she laughed, "but I'm not that disciplined, much to the disappointment of my Jewish studies professor, Anil, my Palestinian friends, and Christopher the Indian pastor. They are all like, 'What's your problem?'"

We talked more as we ate Indian food and then hurried to the mosque, trying to get there before the 8:30 evening prayers.

As we passed a side street, Kristin pointed out the location of an apartment she used to share with some girlfriends from the 24/7 prayer ministry. They named their home WiFi network "Daughters of the Most High God." Their bird's name was Paraclete.[1]

Kristin said her generation lives in a globalized world, so the idea of learning from other cultures is natural. She said she cherishes coexistence, that she could live beside Muslims and Jews. To coexist is a gift, she said, "and at the same time to desire for them to come into relationship with Jesus, while recognizing the beauty that's present in their culture and recognizing the sin in my own faith's journey."

I guessed that for some people, Kristin's exploration of other formats for faith could come across as a trip through a religious amusement park. Kristin told me she tries to make sure she's not playing games. She enters into chants, prayers, and meditation as sincere expressions of her worship of God. "It has to be authentic," she told me. "Otherwise we are playing dress-up and being fake."

When I watched her face as she delivered that mantra in the temple, I knew she was singing it from her heart.

I also reminded myself that for Kristin this kind of activity is not some peripheral entertainment. "I understand Jesus better when I see Him interact with Hindus and when I see Him interact with Muslims," she told me. She believes that Jesus provides the only way to be saved, but she admitted that white evangelical Christianity is one of her least favorite forms of following Jesus. "Contextualization allows me to find beauty in other cultures and truth in other faiths," she said, "without compromising the reality that Jesus is hope."

I wondered how other young adults could find some of the vitality in other expressions of faith that Kristin has discovered. I asked her for her thoughts about that. She imagined what it could look like if a Protestant fellowship at nearby Loyola University would do a series: "Jesus in Middle Eastern Clothes," "Jesus in Jewish Clothes," and "Jesus in Indian Clothes."

They could make it clear this isn't about making it easy for people to convert, she explained. "It's about God having given gifts to the nations so they would worship Him. There are facets of our understanding of God that we are only going to understand when the gospel is translated not just into another language but into another culture." She guessed that at a college level this kind of revelation could be powerful.

She talked about the church she used to attend back in Colorado and how difficult it would be for them to embrace this kind of learning. "The typical church is scared to death of this stuff," she admitted, "but if they were to actually do it and take it seriously, not only would it enrich their faith and not only would it build a bridge with their friends of other faiths, but it would build a bridge with a post-secular world that is looking for something that holds water."

After a visit to the mosque, Kristin and I said good-bye under the glow of streetlights on a busy corner. She got on one bus and I got on another.

I left Chicago not having seen everything I had hoped to see but having discovered some possible answers to my questions.

Is it true that youth who would never attend a church can find Christ if they can encounter Him outside the traditional Christian format? Jesus People USA shows it can actually work.

Does a respectful, learning-oriented approach toward people who follow other religions actually create life-giving relationships? Erika's friendships seem to provide proof of the bonds that can form.

Can pagan still turn into holy today, even in the United States? Anil's satsang, with its elements transformed from their origin in a Hindu temple, shows that redemption of cultures can happen even now, even in Western nations. His idea of Jesus temples provides another creative model for "a third place."

Can people from other nations who follow Christ outside of traditional Christian culture help a young Western person find an increasingly Christ-centered life? Kristin's crazy Indian-Jewish-urban journey shows that this can really happen.

I didn't see a full-blown revolution, but I could smell something new—and not just from the restaurants I passed on Devon Street.

15

The Man in the End

Can a person become too Jesus centered? I began to wonder that toward the end of my journeys.

In the beginning, as I ventured out to meet people who followed Jesus outside of traditional Christian culture, I was reassured to discover that Jesus had not been sidelined or trivialized. In the satsang in India, the young man sitting cross-legged before me told the story of Jesus walking on the water. After the burning sweetgrass had been passed around the worship circle in Winnipeg, we read that same story. In Thailand, when Mark pulled out the photo the monk carried around, I saw that it was a photo of Jesus. The health-care workers in Bangladesh told me that when the Muslims from the street-sweeper neighborhood gather to learn about the Bible, they hear stories about Jesus. It was the same in the incense-filled room in Chicago; after the chanting and the ringing of the bell, we all listened to the tale of Jesus healing a woman who touched His clothing.

By the end of my travels, I wondered why I wasn't hearing the story of Jeremiah or of the exodus or of the shipwreck of Paul. What about the rest of the Bible? What about the whole story of God?

Particularly in the Hindu world, I grew uncomfortable with the focus on worshiping Sadguru Yeshu. If faith becomes all about single-minded bhakti devotion to Jesus, where do the Father and the Holy Spirit fit in? Are they worshiping a God-man, and that's it?

When I asked a couple of Yeshu Bhaktas about this concern, they gave thoughtful answers. One said he worshiped Jesus as Father, Son, and Holy Spirit. Pradip, the Hindu man who had the motorcycle accident, told me he wants his family to grow in faith as he has done, from a worship of Sadguru Yeshu into a fuller understanding of the one, Triune God.

I realize it's possible that people from a Hindu background can more easily understand the mystery of God than I can. They might be better able to grasp how God can incarnate Himself in a human being, and how He can be one and yet three. My misgivings about their words and their worship may simply stem from the limits of my Western, rigid ways of looking at things.

As I've thought about it more, I've wondered if the adoration of Jesus that I witnessed in the Yeshu Bhaktas presents a call to me to come to a deeper place of love for God in my own life. I wonder, if I spent more time around Yeshu Bhaktas, could they help me enter into a new level of worship of Jesus as fully God and fully man?

I was also told that the believers I visited move on into other parts of the Bible once they've decided to follow Jesus. For them, Jesus provides the best starting point. Anil Yesudas, the leader of the satsang in Chicago, explained that their first goal is to give everyone who attends the meeting a good grasp of the person and work of Jesus. He said they almost always choose Scripture from the four Gospels. If instead they tell stories of Old Testament figures like Abraham or Jacob, the Hindu visitors might say, "This is Islam.

We rejected that." Once they come to faith in Jesus, however, "they can understand the Old Testament as well."

The Liberation of Jesus

As I've dealt with my misgivings about the Jesus emphasis I witnessed on my travels, I've begun to allow myself to simply appreciate what I saw. In fact, I've come to realize that one of the most liberating parts of the movements I studied is right here in this focus on Christ: Jesus Himself enables His followers to get beyond their cultural limitations.

For one thing, He provides common ground. To Muslims, Isa al-Masih is a respected prophet. To many Hindus, Yeshu is divine. To Buddhists, Jesus is an enlightened teacher. He can become the entryway into greater revelation about God.

He also provides the model by which faith spreads to other cultures. In his history of Christianity, Kenneth Scott Latourette wondered why this faith in Jesus so rapidly took over the Roman world and other cultures all over the planet. In some ways, Jesus presents an unlikely figure for this kind of multicultural impact. He lived His life within the limited geography of Palestine. He grew up in a small village. He spent almost all of his time with Jews.

Yet in His emphasis on internals more than externals, Jesus separated faith from a system of ceremonies. Latourette cited several examples. With the woman at the well, Jesus made clear that "salvation is from the Jews," but also freed the woman from Samaritan-versus-Jewish debates about geography. In the future, Jesus said, "true worshipers will worship the Father in Spirit and in truth, for they are the kind of worshipers the Father seeks."[1]

"All of this prepared the way for the universalizing of Christianity," Latourette concluded. Once Jesus broke with a system of rites and ceremonies, "it would be difficult to confine His message to any one race or nation."[2]

Still today, Jesus, who didn't write a book or start an organization, leads people out of rigid adherence to systems or institutions. He's the reason creative personalities continue to pop up to take God's story and help it flourish in new ways for new times and new places.

Jesus freed that faith to express itself within a boundless variety of cultures. This Jesus faith has broken out of the European and American cultural box that has come to define it. We can now see the limitless nature of the creativity the Holy Spirit can bring.

The Centrality of Jesus

There's still more, though, to the Jesus emphasis I experienced. This devotion to Jesus, this adoration of Him, this fixation on Him reminds me of the central place He must have in the faith that bears His name. In some ways, that point seems so obvious it's not even worth stating. Yet it's so easy to have that central place slide over to the side.

One of the revealing things to me about the study Willow Creek Church did of the spiritual state of their members (see chapter 9) was that their first grid for determining maturity didn't look at Christ. They looked at church activity. Busyness in church, though, didn't necessarily equate with spiritual growth.

When they recalibrated their results around a person's relationship with Jesus, they discovered a continuum that made sense. As people moved closer toward Jesus as the center of their lives, they displayed more of the behaviors and attitudes associated with spiritual growth. Increasingly they expressed a love for God and love for people, and were more apt to participate in activities like tithing, sharing their faith, and serving.[3]

Maybe it takes studies like this and trips like the ones I've taken to highlight the most obvious things. Jesus is the gateway, He is the boundary breaker, and He is the center.

And yet there is more.

The Picture of Jesus

I believe that what I have witnessed is not just about Christ transforming the world, as monumental as that is. I believe I have also seen movements that transform Christ. To be more specific, these movements are changing the picture of Christ, the image Christians and people in the world at large have in their minds when they think of Jesus of Nazareth.

I came to this realization in the most concrete way, when I looked at an actual painting. Recently I had the opportunity to meet a well-known Christian artist. He was talking to a small group of students about creativity. He asked us if we would like to see a painting he was working on. When the group said yes, he unceremoniously took a two-foot by four-foot piece of art board that had been facing the wall, turned it around, and placed it on a table.

The image I saw almost made me gasp. It was a portrait of a dark-skinned man with short beard and shoulder-length hair. He could have been a light-skinned African American man or a man from the Middle East or Afghanistan. He was wearing a white robe. The man held his hands in symbolic gestures. On one hand, the palm faced upward and on the hand rested a golden key. The man's other hand, also open, was bent backward, fingers curling forward. On both hands were red scars. Around the man's head was a white glow, and behind that a stylized ring of galaxies and stars.

Clearly this was a painting of Jesus, but a very different sort of Jesus.

After the group session had finished, I asked the artist how he came to paint this picture. He had been painting this man's face, he said, and he saw that the face could represent many different nationalities. "I thought he would make a good face of Christ," he explained. He hoped a face like this would speak to people from a variety of cultures.

Yes, the face spoke to me. As Jesus takes root in Hindu and Muslim cultures, His face will look different. We have seen a blue-eyed, white-skinned Jesus because we have worshiped Jesus from a European and American cultural point of view. As we learn to worship Jesus through the eyes of people from Asia and Africa, we will see a more full-color view of His face. We will come to understand more of who Jesus really is.

In this unfinished painting, I could see a new kind of Jesus. He combined the traditional Christian halo with non-Western skin tones and He expressed Himself through Asian mudra-style hand positions.

In this book I've compared these new movements to the importing of new recipes and aromas into our cuisine. Another metaphor could be the adding of more colors to the picture of Jesus Himself.

Some of the people I met told me how their picture of Jesus has changed. As Cal and I drove through Bangladesh, he reflected on his fifteen years in the country and told me, "My faith has completely changed. The core of my faith is Jesus. I knew He wasn't a white Westerner. Now I know some of the ways He isn't like a white Westerner."

In the West, Cal learned about Christ from the top down. He thought of Him as Logos, as Creator. "We start Him off as God and we learn about Him as a man," Cal commented. "Whereas here, He's a man. And you learn about Him as God." He said he has learned to put the dust back on Jesus. He has learned more about the humanity of Christ, how Jesus knows what tears are like, what hunger is like.

On a little street in an Indian city, I looked up at the sign for a Christ-centered ashram. Their faith symbol wasn't a cross. It was two pierced feet. Those feet are the feet of their Sadguru, the God-man come to take away the darkness. That's a different picture too.

Finding Jesus

A more complete picture of Jesus allows Jesus to become even more compelling. We can find Him more attractive, and so can others.

These movements have a lot to do with accessibility. For young people in the West, as well as Hindus, Muslims, Buddhists, and tribal peoples around the world, the culture of Christianity has created an unnecessary barrier for them to investigate and follow Jesus. How can these movements create new entryways for people to find Christ? How can they help believers discover more of God?

I believe the principles that emerge from the movements I studied have the potential to reveal those new doorways, those new pathways.

Perhaps if the label "Christian" is not seen as a requirement, new possibilities might appear.

The Bible itself, if studied and discussed with others, has more to say than we often give it credit for. How could we speak out loud the stories of the Bible in our secondary-orality culture?

How can we invite nonbelievers to discover biblical truth with us, meeting them in their settings, making room for their doubts, learning from their perspectives, allowing them to join us in service and obedience?

How could we grapple together with the implications of Jesus's main teaching, the kingdom of God? How could these concepts provide new vocabulary and new conversations?

In our own culture, how can we create new pathways by redeeming pagan rituals?

How could dance provide a format for meeting?

How can we control people less and trust the Holy Spirit more?

Can we go as learners to people of other faiths, eager to understand the truths that God might have revealed to them? As such, how can we work together toward common goals?

What can happen in the midst of such experiments? We can discover new words, new places, new postures, new partnerships, and much more.

It will require risk to try some of these non-American, non-European ideas. It will probably seem silly and uncomfortable at first.

If you would like to venture outside your own cultural boundaries, or if you would like to help a loved one find their way back to Jesus, a next step might involve visiting your loved one in the place where he or she likes to hang out, attending a powwow, worshiping with people from another culture (or with an African American church if you aren't African American yourself), or trying something like a Christ-centered yoga group. Or maybe call together a small group to go through the Bible study at the back of this book. That study will enable you to dream together with others.

Has God put something creative on your heart? In what dream (asleep or awake) has Jesus come calling to you? How has your history, your culture, your training, your experience uniquely equipped you for this risky effort?

If you do try something, I'd like to hear from you. You can reach me at www.bryanbishop.net.

Perhaps the best step to take next would be to stop your reading for a moment and pray. Maybe you would like to bow down and intercede for someone you care about who has drifted away from their faith. Whether you pray now or later, the next time you pray, as a sign of respect for the presence of God, and as a symbol of your willingness to take off the wrappings of European culture, I recommend that you take off your shoes.

The Jesus Story

My own perspective changed as I traveled. I found that as I interviewed more people and visited more groups, the ideas I started with about strategy became less important. One event in particular forced me to see differently.

In Bangladesh, after Cal and I crossed the river, I spent the first night at the farmhouse of a man called Rajib. When morning finally came and I could crawl off my plywood bed, Cal and I talked about our day. Due to his decision the night before to leave a day early, we had to change our plans for the morning. Rajib had some friends he wanted Cal to visit. But Cal also had to meet another man before he left. Cal told me we would have to split up.

Since Rajib didn't speak English and I didn't speak Bengali, this was a worrisome thought. Up until now, Cal had been both my guide and translator. Cal told me just to smile and make the most of it.

After our breakfast and a morning meeting with Rajib's family, a couple of men showed up with motorcycles. I said good-bye and slid onto the back of one of the bikes. Rajib got on the other one, and we set off.

After traversing a creaky reed bridge, we turned onto a path I hadn't been on before. I had thought we would reach Rajib's friends fairly soon, possibly at another farmhouse nearby. Instead the motorcycles kept buzzing along atop the sandy, narrow roadway.

At first, I just enjoyed the view. Like many of the single-lane dirt roads in this area, we were traveling about eight feet above the watery fields, which stretched out on either side of us. I watched two cows munching on a stack of hay. We passed women carrying bundles, their bright saris flowing in the breeze. One mud bank led down to a swimming hole. A wet boy looked up in wonder as we went by.

After about an hour had passed, I began to allow myself to think about the vulnerable position I was in. I had no idea where I was. I was at the mercy of people I had met only one day before. If I had to ask these people for anything, I couldn't. I wasn't sure where they were taking me or why they were taking me there.

We made a couple of turns and entered a village. Finally, we stopped. I looked at the white-walled building in front of us and recognized the name of the little aid organization we had visited earlier. This must be an outpost office, I thought.

I was ushered into the small cement building, past a little courtyard, and into a bright green office. After I sat down, many more people crowded in until twelve of us were squeezed together.

Rajib sat behind the desk. He spoke to me with a lot of earnest Bengali words.

Soon a guest arrived. He introduced himself in pretty good English and told me he was a teacher at a local high school.

Now I could finally understand what Rajib was so adamantly trying to get through to me. As the teacher translated, Rajib told me that a jamaat met in this office. "In this area," he said, "two hundred people here are interested in Isa. They want and need Christ!" He looked at me intently.

"You are the first Christian missionary who has come to this area," Rajib told me. "These people need a teacher. They need a shepherd."

As if on cue, the high school teacher added, "I like Isa because His teachings are very helpful for any person."

As Rajib continued to sweeten his offer, saying they were not interested in money, saying how welcome I would be if I moved here, I tried to come up with a good way to respond.

Immediately I thought of all the reasons Rajib's idea wouldn't work. All these people in this office and all the two hundred others Rajib had spoken about, they probably identified themselves as Muslim followers of Isa. There were no Christians at all in this whole area. Although their interest in Isa might cause distress for their families, they had a reasonably good chance of following Jesus within their own community. Pioneers like Rajib had faced the brunt of the persecution. Now that there were several followers of Isa in this area, their prospects of surviving family pressure were pretty good. But if somebody like me, a white, Western Christian, showed up to lead these jamaats, the believers would quickly become identified with a foreign culture and religion. The natural flow of witness along family relationships would most likely slow to a trickle.

Someone with Western theological training could probably give them some valuable knowledge. But as I looked at Rajib and I thought about his fervor for the Bible and the study he had done with Tripon, I also thought he wasn't giving himself and all the others enough credit. I wanted Rajib to value the ways God was already leading them through the Bible and through the Holy Spirit. But how to say all this in this room full of people?

Rajib paused and stared at me, expectantly. Suddenly I remembered the story I had read that morning, sitting on the bed under my mosquito net.

"The disciples of Isa were young men," I said. "Several of them were fishermen. Isa wanted them to understand if they gave Him what they had, He could make it enough."

I watched the eyes in the room focus on my lips and then turn to look at the translator as he spoke.

"You know the story," I continued, "about the time when Jesus had taught the people and a huge crowd gathered. There were five thousand men there as well as women and children."

The men in the room bent their heads forward to watch me and listen to the teacher. I told about how evening was approaching and the disciples asked Jesus to dismiss the crowd so the people could go and get dinner.

In telling the story, I intended to make the point that Rajib's strategy of bringing in a Christian expert was going to do more harm than good. I wanted him to realize how many gifts they already had among themselves. I wanted them to see how Jesus Himself relied on simple disciples. I had intended to briefly summarize a well-known story and then make my point. As I spoke, though, I looked at the faces in the room and I didn't see the recognition in them that I expected.

I continued, "Jesus turned to His disciples and said, 'You give them something to eat.'" When the translator had relayed my words, I noticed some of the eyes getting wider. I realized, some of the people here have never heard this story!

I slowed down and added more details, cherishing the moment. Suddenly my point didn't really matter to me anymore. If my observation was correct, I had the opportunity to bring the people in this room onto a hillside with me in Palestine and I could help them witness, many for the first time, a miracle done by a man some people thought was an ordinary rabbi. But rabbis and prophets don't do miracles like this. That, I thought, was the real point.

This journey, in the end, is not about a strategy. It's not about new methods. It's not even about culture. It's about a person. It's about a person who leads us out of the ruts we're in. It's about a movement that has discovered how to worship this person in the midst of non-European, non-American cultures. It's about a Jesus-centered revolution in creative expression, a revolution that is only just beginning.

Appendix

Boundless Jesus Bible Study

The Boundless Jesus Bible Study gives groups a chance to experience many of the principles in this book. Through short videos available on www.BoundlessJesus.com, they can hear a bhajan, they can watch a powwow, or they can bow in prayer using an ancient format called *Agpia*. The study helps them interact with the Bible as oral stories and it provides a taste of different cultural styles of worship and discussion. It allows groups to envision together how some of the boundary-breaking aspects of Jesus's life could impact their lives, their families, and their neighborhoods.

How to Use the Bible Study

The study consists of ten sessions, which follow the themes of the chapters of *Boundless*. Groups can use the study as a way to discuss the content of this book. Each session contains a few optional discussion questions for this purpose. But the Bible study can also be used without those book-related discussion questions. It's not necessary for participants to read *Boundless*. It's not even necessary for participants to have made commitments to Christ. The sessions provide nonbelievers a chance to ask their questions in a safe and accessible environment.

Time and Work Required

Each session will take approximately an hour and a half. Before the session starts, groups can begin with a meal or some other community-building activity.

The study does not require group homework, other than reading this book if the group is using the study as a way to discuss *Boundless*. The group facilitator, though, will need to do a little preparation before each week's discussion begins. It's very important for group facilitators to go to www.BoundlessJesus.com and watch the videos and read the instructions for Boundless Jesus Bible Study facilitators. It will take approximately thirty minutes to go through this material. The facilitators should also print out the "Facilitator's Guide." Group members can take turns facilitating, but each facilitator should go through this preparation material.

A Typical Session

Almost all of the sessions contain the following elements:

- 10 minutes: Review the story from the previous meeting. Some groups may want to retell the story by acting it out or by drawing a picture.
- 10 minutes: An introduction to the topic for the current session. These are often short videos or slide shows.
- 45 minutes: Learning and discussing a Bible story.
- 15 minutes: Personal sharing.
- 10 minutes: Prayer.

Bible Storying

At the heart of each session is the Bible story itself. Group members will learn the stories in a way that will enable them to tell the stories to others.

One principle of the Bible storying approach is to keep the discussion focused almost entirely on the story for that week. If all the group members have a lot of previous Bible knowledge, they can bring in other Bible verses or historical facts in their discussion. As quickly as possible, though, the discussion should return to the story at hand. If many group members are new believers or nonbelievers, it's best to stick only to the facts of the story. In such groups, members should make their points using only elements of the story itself. This principle allows the group to approach the Bible in a way that would not alienate anyone, even someone who has had no previous exposure to the Bible.

Learning and discussing each Bible story involves seven steps. In each of the sessions, the facilitator will lead the group through these steps.

1. Read the story once. One member of the group will read the story.
2. Take two minutes to silently look over the story.
3. Tell the story to each other. Group members will pair up. Each will attempt to tell the story to the other person. The intention isn't to memorize the story word for word or to comment on the story. It's simply to tell the parts of the story each person remembers. This should take approximately one minute per person.
4. Dig deeper into the story. The facilitator will ask questions to help the group get into the story. First, the questions will simply unpack what happened. Where did this event take place? What happened next? Who spoke first? Then the questions will turn more to analysis. Why do you think this person

said that? In the story, this person chose to do this, but what else could she have chosen to do?

5. Make personal applications from the story. Now the facilitator will move to questions like: Have you or someone you know ever faced a situation like this? Can you relate to this character in what he chose to do?

6. Tell your own stories. In answering the application questions, participants can share their own stories that relate to the lessons from the Bible.

7. Retell the story. During the days between meetings, group members look for opportunities to tell the story to another person. Each meeting will begin with time to tell the story from the last meeting.

Session One: Wise Men

The beginning: As the group gathers, they will take off their shoes. For almost every one of the Boundless Jesus Bible Study sessions, group members will remove their shoes. The group leader will read the introductory material from the Facilitator's Guide.

The story: Matthew 2:1–12. The group facilitator will use discussion questions from the Facilitator's Guide to help the group dig into the story.

The discussion: Take turns sharing observations or prayer requests, and pray for each other. The facilitator will encourage group members to look for opportunities to tell the story and to come prepared to retell the story at the next meeting.

For *Boundless* book discussion: In chapters 1 and 2, the author tells about people who are following Jesus outside of Western Christianity. How do these present-day stories compare to the story of the wise men? How do they seem similar or different?

Session Two: John's Disciples Follow Jesus

The beginning: Group members will enter and will take off their shoes. The facilitator will ask members to gather in a circle. If the room allows it, and if group members feel comfortable doing so, they will sit on the floor. The facilitator will place a candle on a plate in the center of the group.

The group will begin by reviewing the story of the wise men. Someone will volunteer to retell the story, or the group will retell it together.

The facilitator will explain that this session will focus on the Hindu world. The group will watch a short video.

The story: John 1:32–42. The group facilitator will use discussion questions from the Facilitator's Guide to help the group dig into the story.

The discussion: The group will share prayer requests and will pray for each other.

For *Boundless* book discussion: In this story, we've looked at what it meant for John's disciples to follow Jesus. Chapter 3 shows people following Jesus within Hinduism. How do you think their decisions to follow Jesus are similar to or different from the decisions John's disciples made? What questions does this raise for you?

Session Three: Crowds Begin to Follow

The beginning: Review the previous story. The facilitator will then explain *Agpia*, an ancient Coptic form of prayer. If the group has the space and the health for this, they will use the Agpia slide show to enter into the words and the movements of this prayer form.

The story: Matthew 4:23–25. The group facilitator will use discussion questions from the Facilitator's Guide to help the group dig into the story.

The discussion: Sharing and prayer.

For *Boundless* book discussion: As we've bowed and as we've reflected on how people responded to Jesus as He began His ministry, we can now also think about how Muslims perceive Jesus. How do you think a Muslim might view the story we've just read? How do you think a Muslim who has come to biblical faith in Jesus would view the story?

Session Four: Jesus Raises a Widow's Son

The beginning: Review the previous story. The facilitator will then show the group a few slides of Buddhist temples and rituals.

The story: Luke 7:11–17. The group facilitator will use discussion questions from the Facilitator's Guide to help the group dig into the story.

The discussion: Sharing and prayer.

For *Boundless* book discussion: Based on the author's descriptions of Buddhism in chapter 5, how do you think Buddhists might understand or misunderstand Jesus in the story we just read?

Session Five: Walking on Water

The beginning: The group will arrange furniture to enable them to sit in a circle. They will review the previous story. The facilitator will begin this session with a few facts about Native Americans. Then the group will watch a short clip of a powwow.

The story: Matthew 14:22–33. The group facilitator will use discussion questions from the Facilitator's Guide to help the group dig into the story.

The discussion: When it comes time for the group to make personal applications from the story, the group will pass a small rock.

Each person can give their thoughts while they have the stone in their hand. The other group members must listen quietly and not interrupt the person with the stone. After going around the circle, the group can repeat the process, sharing anything they want to say about their week or about a prayer need. The group will close in prayer.

For *Boundless* book discussion: Chapter 6 features this story about walking on water. If the powwow dancers pray to Jesus before they dance, and if the intention of a dancer is to worship the Creator in his or her dance, do you think the powwow can be a form of worship? What do you think about the use of dance in worship?

Session Six: The Mustard Seed, the Yeast, the Treasure, and the Pearl

The beginning: After reviewing the previous story, the facilitator will begin by asking someone in the group to briefly tell their story about how they came to faith in Christ and how they feel their journey is going today.

The story: Matthew 13:31–33, 44–46. The group facilitator will use discussion questions from the Facilitator's Guide to help the group dig into the story.

The discussion: In the discussion, the facilitator will encourage others to share about where they are in their faith journey. The group will pray for each other.

For *Boundless* book discussion: This discussion will cover the whole of part 2, Boundary Breakers—chapters 7–11. Chapter 9 deals with process and uses the kingdom of God to explain the journey of faith. How could you use the kingdom circles to describe your own journey?

Session Seven: Mary Anoints Jesus

The beginning: After reviewing the previous story, the facilitator will lead the group in a simple breathing exercise that is described in the Facilitator's Guide.

The story: John 12:1–8. The group facilitator will use discussion questions from the Facilitator's Guide to help the group dig into the story.

The discussion: Sharing and prayer.

For *Boundless* book discussion: Mary expressed her feelings about Jesus in an extravagant way. Chapter 12 presents many ways to follow Jesus. Do you ever have the desire to follow Jesus extravagantly? If so, which ideas, if any, from chapter 12 appealed to you? Did chapter 12 or this discussion today make you think of some other ways to apply the concepts of this book?

Session Eight: Zacchaeus

The beginning: The group will review the previous story. The facilitator will also read some statistics about the increasing percentage of young people in the United States, Canada, and Europe who do not want to affiliate with any religious group. The facilitator will ask if members of the group know of any people like this.

The story: Luke 19:1–10. The group facilitator will use discussion questions from the Facilitator's Guide to help the group dig into the story.

The discussion: In addition to the other concerns group members share, the facilitator will encourage the group to pray about people they know who have drifted away from faith in Christ. The group will also make arrangements for the places they will meet in their next session.

For *Boundless* book discussion: So far in *Boundless*, you've been exposed to many different people who have chosen to follow Jesus outside of what we commonly think of as Christian culture. Chapter 13 presents the views of people who agree and disagree with these approaches. In the story of Zacchaeus, Jesus says He came to seek and save the lost. As we think about God's desire to seek and save Muslims, Hindus, and Buddhists, what do you think He wants to say to them? What do you think they need to change in order to follow Him? What do you think the world needs most?

Session Nine: Thomas Believes

The beginning: For this session the group will meet in a public place. It might be a park, a restaurant, or a coffee shop. Larger groups will split into subgroups as small as two or three people depending on the space restrictions of the public place. The facilitator will prepare other facilitators in advance to lead each of the smaller groups. This is the one study in which group members don't have to take off their shoes! They will begin by reviewing the previous story.

The story: John 20:24–29. The group facilitators will use discussion questions from the Facilitator's Guide to help the group dig into the story.

The discussion: Even groups who are not studying *Boundless* will reflect on the *Boundless* application questions. They will write down their answers to those questions and will take those ideas to the next meeting.

For general discussion and *Boundless* book discussion: In chapter 14, the author gives a picture of many kinds of faith in one city. As you look around at the people in this room or in this park, and as you think about doubt and faith, in what ways can you imagine faith reaching out beyond the church walls of your community?

Brainstorm about what that could look like and how you could be involved.

Session Ten: Feeding the Five Thousand

The beginning: Start with a longer review than normal. The facilitator will help the group reflect back on all the stories so far.

The story: Mark 6:30–44. The group facilitator will use discussion questions from the Facilitator's Guide to help the group dig into the story.

The discussion: For this concluding session, all groups, even those not studying the book *Boundless*, will reflect on the *Boundless* study group's closing questions.

For general discussion and *Boundless* book discussion: In chapter 15, the author closes *Boundless* with a scene in which he tells the story of the feeding of the five thousand. What have you learned about Bible storying through this study? How have you already used these stories? How would you like to use them? Share as a group the plans and dreams you came up with last week. If Jesus said, "You feed them," what would you say? What could you say you have? Conclude by praying for each other, for ideas or plans made in the last meeting, and for the ability to continue learning and telling the Bible's stories.

Notes

Chapter 1 The Man in the Beginning

1. Randy is a pseudonym. Like many of the people I interviewed for this book, Randy agreed to talk with me on the condition that I would not disclose his true identity. To make it easier to keep the real names separate from the made-up names, in this book when I introduce a person by their first name only, I'm usually using a pseudonym. If I use both first and last names, I'm usually using a real name.

2. David B. Barrett, George T. Kurian, and Todd M. Johnson, eds., *World Christian Encyclopedia: A Comparative Survey of Churches and Religions in the Modern World* (New York: Oxford University Press, 2001).

3. Acts 2:1–41.

4. Ralph Winter, "Editorial Comment," *Mission Frontiers* (September/October 1996), 2.

5. John Travis, "Messianic Muslim Followers of Isa," *International Journal of Frontier Mission* (Spring 2000), 54.

6. Ibid.

7. Acts 24:14.

8. "'Nones' on the Rise," The Pew Forum on Religion and Public Life, October 9, 2012, http://www.pewresearch.org.

9. "Religion among the Millennials," The Pew Forum on Religion and Public Life, February 17, 2010, http://www.pewforum.org.

10. David Kinnaman and Gabe Lyons, *unChristian: What a New Generation Really Thinks about Christianity and Why It Matters* (Grand Rapids: Baker, 2007), 26.

Chapter 2 A Taste of Something New

1. "'Nones' on the Rise," http://www.pewresearch.org.

2. "'Unchurched' on the Rise?" Gallup, March 26, 2002; and "Democrats More Liberal, Less White than in 2008," Gallup, November 7, 2011, http://www.gallup.com.

3. "Most Britons, Canadians 'Unchurched,'" Gallup, October 18, 2005, http://www.gallup.com.

4. "'Nones' on the Rise," http://www.pewresearch.org.

5. "U.S. Religious Landscape Survey," The Pew Forum on Religion and Public Life, February 2008, http://www.pewforum.org.

6. "In U.S., Rise in Religious 'Nones' Slows in 2012," Gallup, January 10, 2013, http://www.gallup.com.

7. "Americans Divided on the Importance of Church," Barna Group, March 25, 2014, http://www.barna.org.

8. Frank Viola and George Barna, *Pagan Christianity?: Exploring the Roots of Our Church Practices* (Ventura: BarnaBooks, 2008), xxvi.

9. Ibid., xxvii.

10. Roland Allen, *Missionary Methods: St Paul's or Ours?* (Grand Rapids: Eerdmans, 1997), 142.

11. Charles H. Kraft, ed., *Appropriate Christianity* (Pasadena: William Carey Library, 2005), 15.

12. Ibid., 17.

13. Mike W. Stroop, "Insider Movements—Outsider Witness" (paper presented at Rethinking Forum, Minneapolis, 2008).

14. For a partial list of verses supporting this, see "Appendix A: 'All Nations' Verse List," Impact Eternity, http://www.impacteternity.com/eng-appendixes.htm.

15. Kinnaman and Lyons, *unChristian*, 123.

16. John Stott, quoted in Phil Parshall, *New Paths in Muslim Evangelism: Evangelical Approaches to Contextualization* (Grand Rapids: Baker, 1980), 157–58.

Chapter 3 The Satsang

1. Aradhna, "Deep Jale," *Deep Jale,* 2000, CD; see http://www.aradhnamusic.com.

2. See also H. L. Richard, *Hinduism* (Pasadena: William Carey Library, 2007), 14.

3. Jason Mandryk, *Operation World,* 7th ed. (Colorado Springs: Biblica, 2010), 411.

4. Ibid., 414.

5. Swami Dayanand Bharati, *Living Water and Indian Bowl* (Pasadena: William Carey Library, 2004), 94; see also pages 7 and 80.

6. Bhagavad Gita 9:32, 18:64, 65 and 12:6, 7. According to H. L. Richard, in the Gita, Krishna clearly claims "that not only the high-caste person but even the low-caste person, even the woman who has devotion to me, will come to me. It means not to reincarnation but to God and eternity."

7. Mandryk, *Operation World,* 412.

8. Herbert E. Hoefer, *Churchless Christianity* (Pasadena: William Carey Library, 1991), 96.

Chapter 4 The Jamaat

1. Mandryk, *Operation World,* 134.

2. Ibid.

3. Surah 3:84; 9:70; 21:105; 23:49.

4. Abdullah Yusuf Ali, trans., *The Qur'an* (Elmhurst: Tahrike Tarsile Qur'an, 2008).

5. Surah 3:35–52; 19:2–35.

6. Surah 3:45; 4:171.

7. Don M. McCurry, "Cross-Cultural Models for Muslim Evangelism," *Missiology* 4, no. 3 (1976), 280.

8. H. Byron Earhart, ed., *Religious Traditions of the World* (New York: HarperCollins, 1993), 641.

9. Richard Jameson and Nick Scalevich, "First-Century Jews and Twentieth-Century Muslims," *International Journal of Frontier Mission* (Spring 2000), 56.

10. Warren C. Chastain, "Should Christians Pray the Muslim *Salat?*" *International Journal of Frontier Mission* (July–September 1995), 164.

11. Jameson and Scalevich, "First-Century Jews and Twentieth-Century Muslims," 35.

Chapter 5 The Monk

1. Martin Palmer, *The Jesus Sutras: Rediscovering the Lost Scrolls of Taoist Christianity* (New York: Ballantine Books, 2001), 4?

2. Ibid., 173.

3. Ibid., 226.

4. Ibid., 214.

5. Ibid., 161.

6. Ibid., 195.

7. Ibid., 202–3.

8. Ibid., 163.

9. Ibid., 63.

10. David Burnett, *The Spirit of Buddhism: A Christian Perspective on Buddhist Thought* (London: Monarch, 1996), 271.

11. Ibid.

12. Palmer, *The Jesus Sutras,* 253.

13. Earhart, ed., *Religious Traditions of the World,* 858–59.

14. Pali is a language originating in India that was used for many of the early Buddhist scriptures. It is still used as a Theravada Buddhist liturgical language.

15. John R. Davis, *Poles Apart: Contextualizing the Gospel in Asia* (Bangalore: Theological Book Trust, 1993), 141.

16. Ibid.

17. Ibid., 46.

18. Ibid., 45.

19. Ibid., 192; see also "Christian Communications Institute (CCI)—Payap University," *Thai Christian Foundation,* 2013, http://thaichristianfoundation.org/program/christian-communications-institute.

20. Davis, *Poles Apart,* 191.

Chapter 6 The Powwow

1. "Letters Written by Those at Sand Creek," http://www.colorado.edu/csilw/sandcreekltrs.htm.

2. Charles Eastman, *The Essential Charles Eastman (Ohiyesa): Light on the Indian World,* ed. Michael Oren Fitzgerald (Bloomington: World Wisdom, 2007), 156–57.

3. Ibid., 164.

4. Ibid., 15.

5. Ibid., 192.

6. Ibid., 193.

7. Ibid., 37.

8. Dave and Neta Jackson, *Exiled to the Red River* (Bloomington: Bethany, 2003), 15.

9. Eastman, *The Essential Charles Eastman*, 2.

10. Ibid., 50.

11. Richard Twiss, *One Church Many Tribes: Following Jesus the Way God Made You* (Ventura: Regal, 2000), 45.

12. Ibid., 46.

13. Public Broadcasting Service, *Religion and Ethics News Weekly* (June 17, 2008).

14. Twiss, *One Church Many Tribes*, 80.

15. Mandryk, *Operation World*, 867.

16. Twiss, *One Church Many Tribes*, 39.

17. Ibid., 35.

18. Ibid., 83.

Chapter 8 Put the Book in Its Place

1. "Bible Engagement in Churchgoers' Hearts, Not Always Practiced," LifeWay Research, September 6, 2012, www.lifewayresearch.com.

2. "Six in Ten Americans Read Bible at Least Occasionally," Gallup, October 20, 2000, www.gallup.com.

3. "The Reading of the Scriptures," Catholic Biblical Federation, 2008, reported in Sandro Magister, "Reading the Bible, Who, What, When, Where, How, Why," April 30, 2008, http://chiesa.espresso.repubblica.it.

4. "Who Knows What about Religion," Pew Research, September 28, 2010, http://www.pewforum.org.

5. Gary M. Burge, "The Greatest Story Never Read," *Christianity Today*, August 9, 1999, http://www.christianitytoday.com.

6. "American 'Millennials' are Spiritually Diverse," LifeWay Research, April 27, 2010, http://www.lifewayresearch.com; see also Barna Research Group, "What Do Americans Really Think About the Bible?," March 27, 2013, http://www.barna.org. In this study, youth aged 18–28 reported a higher interest than older respondents in receiving teaching from the Bible about issues like sexuality, family conflict, death, and illness.

7. "Making Disciples of Oral Learners," Lausanne Committee for World Evangelization, October 2006, http://www.lausanneworldpulse.com.

8. Marshall McLuhan, *Understanding Media: The Extensions of Man* (Cambridge: MIT Press, 1998), 82, quoted in A. Steven Evans, "What Happens When the Literate Stop Reading?," http://media1.imbresources.org/files/83/8363/8363-46136.pdf.

9. Evans, "What Happens When the Literate Stop Reading?," http://media1.imbresources.org/files/83/8363/8363-46136.pdf.

10. "National Assessment of Adult Literacy," NAAL, 2003, http://nces.ed.gov.

11. "Adult Literacy and Lifeskills Survey," Institute of Education Sciences, 2003, http://nces.ed.gov.

12. Grant Lovejoy, "Chronological Bible Storying: Description, Rationale and Implications" (paper presented at Non-Print Media Consultation in Nairobi, Kenya, June 2000), as excerpted in "A Brief History of Chronological Bible Storying," Echo the Story, http://www.echothestory.com.
13. Matthew 13:10.
14. Mark 4:34.
15. Michael Novelli, "Changed by the Story," *Immerse*, 2010, 7–11.
16. Tommy Jones, *Postmodern Youth Ministry* (Grand Rapids: Zondervan, 2001), 27, as quoted in A. Steven Evans, "What Happens When the Literate Stop Reading?," http://media1.imbresources.org/files/83/8363/8363-46136.pdf.
17. For more of Bryan Thompson's teaching on storying, or to sign up for his podcast, go to http://www.story4all.com.
18. Eugene Peterson, *The Message: The Bible in Contemporary Language* (Colorado Springs: NavPress, 2005), 1164.

Chapter 9 Move Toward Jesus

1. Paul G. Hiebert, *Anthropological Reflections on Missiological Issues* (Grand Rapids: Baker, 1994), 107–36.
2. Michael Frost and Alan Hirsch, *The Shaping of Things to Come: Innovation and Mission for the 21st-Century Church* (Peabody, MA: Hendrickson, 2003), 47.
3. Bounded set: 1 John 4:5–6; Luke 11:23; 2 Corinthians 5:17; John 1:12. Centered set: 1 John 4:7; Luke 9:50; 1 Corinthians 7:17–24; John 18:37. For a discussion of how to balance the Bible's teaching on bounded and centered sets, see Tim Harmon, "Who's In and Who's Out? Christianity and Bounded Sets vs. Centered Sets," Western Seminary, January 17, 2014, http://www.westernseminary.edu/trans formedblog/2014/01/17/whos-in-and-whos-out-christianity-and-bounded-sets-vs -centered-sets.
4. "Key Findings," REVEAL, 2009, http://www.revealnow/key_findings.asp.
5. Ibid.
6. Ibid.
7. Ibid.
8. Ibid.
9. E. Stanley Jones, *Good News Magazine*, 1970.
10. Roland Allen, *Missionary Methods*, 149.
11. 1 Corinthians 8:9.
12. Allen, *Missionary Methods*, 118.
13. Ibid., 145.
14. See "Six Reasons Young Christians Leave Church," Barna Group, September 28, 2011, http://www.barna.org/teens-next-gen-articles/528-six-reasons -young-christians-leave-church.
15. David Kinnaman and Aly Hawkins, *You Lost Me: Why Young Christians are Leaving Church . . . and Rethinking Faith* (Grand Rapids: Baker Books, 2011).

Chapter 10 Turn Pagan into Holy

1. "Christmas," A&E Television Networks, July 27, 2012, http://www.history .com/topics/Christmas.

2. Edwin and Jennifer Woodruff Tait, "Why Do We Have Christmas Trees?" *Christianity Today,* December 11, 2008, http://www.christianitytoday.com/ch /thepastinthepresent/storybehind/whychristmastrees.html.

3. "Christmas," http://www.history.com/topics/Christmas.

4. John R. Davis, *Poles Apart: Contextualizing the Gospel in Asia* (India: Theological Book Trust, 1993), 137.

5. Frank Viola and George Barna, *Pagan Christianity?: Exploring the Roots of our Church Practices* (Ventura: BarnaBooks, 2008), 104.

6. Steve Russo, *Why Celebrate Easter* (Nashville: B & H Publishing, 2001), 6.

7. John H. Walton, Victor H. Matthews, and Mark W. Chavalas, *The IVP Bible Background Commentary: Old Testament* (Downers Grove, IL: InterVarsity, 2000), 48.

8. Ibid., 49.

9. Numbers 24:1; see comment in Walton, Matthews, and Chavalas, *The IVP Bible Background Commentary,* 161–62: "As a Mesopotamian prophet, Balaam's usual procedures when invoking a god or seeking an omen would have been to engage in some form of divination."

10. S. N. Wald, "Christian Terminology in Hindi," *Missionstudien* (vol. 1, 1962), 231, quoted in Swami Dayanand Bharati, *Living Water and Indian Bowl* (Pasadena: William Carey Library, 2004), 97.

11. Matthew 15:1–20.

12. Galatians 5:1.

13. Shukavak N. Dasa, "A Hindu Primer," Sanskrit Religions Institute, 2007, http://www.sanskrit.org/www/Hindu%20Primer/samskaras.html.

14. Amy Roemer, ed., *Go Manual* (Seattle: YWAM, 2012), 136.

Chapter 11 Seek the Whole Truth

1. "Gajendra Moksha: The Story of the Elephant's King," Riiti, March 12, 2014, http://www.riiti.com/587/gajendra_moksha_the_story_of_elephants_king.

2. John 21:4–6.

3. This fact is substantiated by Mandryk, *Operation World,* 407.

4. "Daniel 1," Bible Hub, http://www.biblehub.com./commentaries/guzik/com mentaries/2701.htm.

5. See Daniel 4:8; 1:8; 1:20; 5:11. See also Walton, Matthews, and Chavalas, *The IVP Bible Background Commentary,* 730.

6. Ibid., 729–30.

7. Ibid., 733.

8. Daniel 2:37.

9. Daniel 2:27–28.

10. Luke 7:1–10.

11. Luke 4:24–27.

12. Epimenides of Knossos, "Cretica," quoted in "Epimenides," Wikipedia, March 12, 2014, http://en.wikipedia.org/wiki/Epimenides.

13. Acts 17:27–28.

14. I'm indebted to Dr. Gregory Boyd for his thoughts on this subject, as found in "Is There Truth?"; DVD available at the Y360 store, http://www.y360.org/store.

15. Augustine of Hippo, *On Christian Teaching.* Here's the whole quote: "A person who is a good and true Christian should realize that truth belongs to his

Lord, wherever it is found, gathering and acknowledging it even in pagan literature, but rejecting superstitious vanities and deploring and avoiding those who 'though they knew God did not glorify him as God.'"

16. Samuel M. Zwemer, *The Muslim Christ* (Edinburgh: Oliphant, Anderson & Ferrier, 1912), 8; excerpted at "The Muslim Christ," Truthnet, March 12, 2014, http://www.truthnet.org/islam/Muslimchrist/introduction.

17. C. S. Lewis, *Mere Christianity* (New York: Macmillan, 1952), 43.

18. Ephesians 4:22; Colossians 3:9.

19. Gerald R. McDermott, *Can Evangelicals Learn from World Religions? Jesus, Revelation and Religious Traditions* (Downers Grove, IL: InterVarsity, 2000), 152.

20. Ibid., 209.

21. Ibid., 92.

22. Ibid., 209.

23. David Kinnaman and Aly Hawkins, *You Lost Me: Why Young Christians are Leaving Church . . . And Rethinking Faith* (Grand Rapids: Baker, 2011), 11.

24. Kinnaman and Lyons, *unChristian*, 33.

25. 1 Corinthians 8:1–2.

26. H. L. Richard, "Some Pointers for Personal Evangelism among Educated Hindus," *Mission Frontiers* (September–October 1996), 18.

27. Richard A. Swenson, *More than Meets the Eye: Fascinating Glimpses of God's Power and Design* (Colorado Springs: NavPress, 2000), 102.

28. Ibid., 136.

29. Aradhna, "Amrit Vani," *Amrit Vani*, 2007, CD; see http://www.aradhna music.com.

Chapter 12 Outside the Bun

1. Chris Hale, "Aradhna: From Comfort to Discomfort, from Church to Temple," *International Journal of Frontier Missiology* (Fall 2007), 147.

2. Ibid., 150.

3. John 18:20.

4. Genesis 12:1–3; 18:18; 22:18; 28:14; Galatians 3:8–9.

5. Rick Love, "Blessing the Nations in the 21st Century: A 3D Approach to Apostolic Ministry," *International Journal of Frontier Missiology* (Spring 2008), 34.

6. Ray Oldenburg, *The Great Good Place: Cafes, Coffee Shops, Bookstores, Bars, Hair Salons, and Other Hangouts at the Heart of a Community* (Emeryville, NY: Marlowe & Company, 1999).

7. Hebrews 10:25.

8. George Barna, *Revolution* (Carol Stream, IL: Tyndale, 2005), 114.

9. Eastman, *The Essential Charles Eastman (Ohiyesa)*, 31; see also page 6.

10. Bruce Katz and Jennifer Bradley, "Divided We Sprawl," *Atlantic Monthly* (December 1999), 42, quoted in Ray Oldenburg, ed., *Celebrating the Third Place* (Emeryville, NY: Marlowe & Company, 2001), 4.

11. McDermott, *Can Evangelicals Learn from World Religions?*, 218.

12. "Standing Together," The Christian-Muslim Consultative Group, http://www.thecmcg.org.

13. *Eid* means "festival" in Arabic and usually refers to "Eid al-Fitr," the holiday that celebrates the end of the Islamic fasting month of Ramadan.

14. Richard Waterstone, *India: The Cultural Companion* (New York: Barnes and Noble, 2005), 84–85.

15. Thomas Ryan, *Prayer of Heart and Body: Meditation and Yoga as Christian Spiritual Practice* (Mahwah, NJ: Paulist Press, 1995), 197.

Chapter 13 What the World Needs Now

1. Robert D. Woodberry, "Reclaiming the M-Word: The Legacy of Missions in Non-Western Societies," *International Journal of Frontier Missiology* (Spring 2008), 17.

2. Ibid., 18.

3. Ibid.

4. Mandryk, *Operation World*, 511.

5. Kraft, ed., *Appropriate Christianity*, 11.

6. Bowing: Daniel 6:10; lifting hands in prayer: 1 Timothy 2:8; robe-like clothing: 2 Chronicles 9:4.

7. Georges Houssney, "Muslim Follower of Jesus, Is This Possible?," *Biblical Missiology*, August 8, 2011, http://biblicalmissiology.org.

8. John Travis, "God Is Doing Something New," *Christianity Today*, December, 2009, http://christianitytoday.com/globalconversation/december2009. This online response, part of the Global Conversations series, features a collection of opinions on the article "Muslim Follower of Jesus?" by Joseph Cumming that appeared in the magazine in December 2009.

9. Kraft, ed., *Appropriate Christianity*, 77.

10. Phil Parshall, "Danger! New Directions in Contextualization," *Evangelical Missions Quarterly* (October 1998), 404–10.

11. J. Dudley Woodberry, "To the Muslim I Became Muslim?" *International Journal of Frontier Missiology* (Spring 2007), 27.

12. Gary Corwin, "A Humble Appeal to C5/Insider Movement Muslim Ministry Advocates to Consider Ten Questions," *International Journal of Frontier Missiology* (Spring 2007), 11.

13. Kraft, ed., *Appropriate Christianity*, 31.

14. Gordon Conwell Theological Seminary, "Christianity in Its Global Context, 1970–2020: Society, Religion, and Mission," June 2013, http://www.gordonconwell.edu/resources//Global-Context-of-Christianity.cfm.

15. E. Stanley Jones, *The Christ of the Indian Road* (Nashville: Abingdon Press, 1925), 126.

Chapter 14 Revolution in Chicago

1. *Paraclete* is a Greek word often translated "counselor" or "helper" and applied in the Gospel of John to the Holy Spirit.

Chapter 15 The Man in the End

1. John 4:23.

2. Kenneth S. Latourette, *A History of Christianity, Volume 1: Beginnings to 1500* (New York: HarperOne, 1975), 56.

3. "Key Findings," http://www.revealnow/key_findings.asp.

Glossary

Bhagavad Gita: Popular portion of the Hindu scriptures, part of the epic *Mahabharata*.

bhajan: A Hindu style of worship song, usually expressing love to the divine.

bhakta: One who has chosen the path of bhakti.

bhakti: Devoted worship of the divine; can involve the worship of only one god.

C-Scale (or C-Spectrum): A continuum that describes six different types of Christ-centered communities Muslims either form or join when they follow Jesus. The spectrum depicts a variety of types of fellowships from very Western or traditional (C1 and C2) to ones closely linked in form or identity with the local Muslim community (C4 and C5). This spectrum can also be seen in Hindu, Buddhist, and tribal communities. See chapter 2, p. 31.

carnatic music: a genre of Indian classical music associated with southern India. Most of the music is meant to be sung.

chant: Melodic and rhythmic singing or speaking, usually involving a limited number of notes.

contextualization: The process of accommodating a message and meanings to another cultural setting.

dholak: A hand drum with two heads, one head slightly smaller than the other.

Eid: Means "festival" in Arabic and usually refers to *Eid al-Fitr*, the holiday that celebrates the end of the Islamic fasting month of Ramadan.

imam: A leader of a Muslim community.

insider: Christ-followers who choose to stay within their own culture, including their religious culture, to live out their faith.

Isa al-Masih: The name given to Jesus in the Qur'an; means "Jesus the Messiah."

jal sanskar: Water sacrament ceremony in Hinduism, used as a format for baptism.

jamaat: Means "community" or "assembly" in Arabic. In a spiritual sense, Muslims use the word to describe religious fellowship groups.

khaen: A mouth organ usually made of bamboo, originating in Southeast Asia.

kurta: A long, loose-fitting shirt with either no collar or a stand-up collar, worn by men in Central and South Asia.

Likay: A form of Thai folk drama.

lungi: A skirt-like wrap worn by men and women primarily in hot climates in Asia.

manjira: A pair of small hand cymbals.

mantra: A sacred sound, word, or group of words used to assist in worship or meditation in Hinduism, Buddhism, Taoism, and many other religions.

millennials: The demographic segment of the population that follows Generation X, sometimes defined as those born between 1982 and 2004.

mudras: Spiritual and symbolic gestures usually involving the hands and fingers, found in Buddhism and Hinduism.

nones: The people who, when asked to select their religious affiliation from a list, pick "none."

Operation World: A reference book and prayer guide that contains spiritual analysis and statistics covering all the nations of the world (www.operationworld.org).

Pali: A language originating in India that was used for many of the early Buddhist scriptures. It is still used as a Theravada Buddhist liturgical language.

Parameshwara: The Supreme God, the Absolute Reality. Some Hindu scriptures refer to Shiva or Vishnu as Parameshwara. Some Bible translations into Hindi or Urdu use Parameshwara for "God."

powwow: A Native American gathering usually involving dancing, drumming, singing, and socializing. The gatherings can last from one day to a full week.

puja: Expressions of honor and worship offered in Hinduism and Buddhism.

Qur'an: The sacred text of Islam, which Muslims believe contains the revelation of God given through the angel Gabriel to Muhammad. The chapters of the Qur'an are called suras.

Ramadan: The Islamic month of fasting. During these 29–30 days, Muslims are not supposed to eat food or drink liquids from dawn until sunset.

saag paneer: A South Asian dish containing spinach and *paneer*, a curd cheese.

Sadguru: True, perfect master; can be a God-man, one who takes away the darkness.

sadhu: In Hinduism, a man who has renounced worldly attachments in order to focus on his spiritual practice.

salat: The ritual prostration prayer practiced by many Muslims five times a day.

satsang: A combination of two Sanskrit words, *sat* meaning "truth" and *sanga* meaning "company" or "community"; a common Hindu gathering of people who seek truth, often through reflection on sacred writings.

sheikh: An Arabic term that could mean the leader of a tribe or an Islamic scholar.

smudge: A Native American ceremonial practice involving the burning of herbs. It can have several meanings, such as cleansing or blessing.

sri: A Sanskrit word used in India as a term of respect. When addressing a deity, it could be translated "holy."

storying: Verbal Bible storytelling, used for both evangelism and discipleship.

tabla: Hand drums used predominantly in India, consisting of two drums, each of a slightly different size and tone.

unchurched: People who say they do not attend or belong to a church, synagogue, or mosque.

Yeshu: Jesus.

Yeshu Bhakta: A devotee of Jesus in the bhakti tradition (see *bhakti* above); a name used by some Hindu-background followers of Jesus as a term that describes their religious identity.

Website Resources

www.boundlessjesus.com: the website for this book, with videos, information, and Bible study materials

www.bryanbishop.net: learn more about the author

www.ywam.org: website for Youth With A Mission

www.barna.org: research about the unchurched and other trends

www.ifcentre.com: Indigenous Family Centre in Winnipeg

www.rethinkingforum.com: information for Hindu ministry

www.simplythestory.org: storying resources

www.cissybradyrogers.com: Cissy's workshops, counseling, and yoga instruction

www.ricklove.net: Rick's consulting on intercultural communication and Christian-Muslim relations

www.missionfrontiers.org: Mission Frontiers magazine

www.safcchicago.com: South Asian Friendship Center in Chicago

Acknowledgments

The story of the making of this book is the story of people who came into my life at just the right time and just the right way. This book was a group project. I'm grateful to God for everyone who contributed.

I want to start by thanking Jeff P., the person who first suggested that I write a book on this subject. That was way back in 1998.

Then I'd like to thank all the people who helped me on my journey of discovery. In particular, I want to honor two people I will never forget. Henk DeBruyn and Jeanet Sybenga both lost battles with cancer since I interviewed them for this book. They both learned much from First Nations people, and both of them inspired me with their faith and their humble appreciation for how God can move in the midst of the art and customs of Native Americans. They left an enduring legacy in the Indigenous Family Centre in Winnipeg, and in many people who have been inspired by their example.

Of the many other people who assisted me, some I can name: Craig Suderman, Inchai and Ruth Srisuwan, Paul De Neui, Richard Silversmith, Daniel Willems, Meredith Winston, Rick Brown, Ben Jones, Jim Tebbe, Jose Joseph, Buddy Hoffman, Lisa Patriquin, Cissy Brady-Rogers, Anil Yesudas, Wilbur Stone, Bryan Thompson,

Jon Trott, Georges Houssney, Don McCurry, Dudley Woodberry, Judy H., Larry Hope, Aila Da Silva, Jeff and Tamara Neely, Andy Butcher, John Somers-Harris, Sumeet and Nicole Gulati, Goutam Datta, Gavriel Gefen, Bill C., and Joshua Praburaj. Many other helpful people I cannot name for security reasons, so I'll call them Randy, Jay, EJ Martin, John and Ann Travis, H. L. Richard, Cal, Arun, Pradip, Tripon, Rajib, Carl, Mark and Emily, Joe, George, Navin, Scott and Amy, Kristin, Ahmed, Vivek, Anand and Muskaan, Erika, and N. from YWAM Chicago. I'm so grateful to all of them for the time they took to talk with me, for the people they introduced me to, and for risking so much information in the hands of a stranger. Thanks also to the two people who worked so hard on transcriptions, Enoch Era and Suzan D.

I'm also grateful for everyone who cheered me on. Foremost among these people is Jackie Johnson, who not only helped me get my first clue about the publishing world but also introduced me to Alice Crider, my agent. Alice, in turn, improved my manuscript greatly, brought in the editing expertise of Mick Silva, and then helped open a door for me with Baker. At Baker, special thanks to Chad Allen, who believed in me enough to champion the idea of publishing this book, and to Rebecca Cooper and Mary Suggs for making my manuscript better.

Other noteworthy cheerleaders include my wife, Tamara, who asked me such great questions and who never stopped believing in me, my father and mother, David Zimmerman, Mark Herringshaw, Simon Wolfert, Marilyn McGinnis, and Phil Wuthier. Thanks also to the prayer group that interceded for me along the way, and to all those who read the manuscript and improved it. Thanks also to all the generous people who pray for me and support me in my work.

Finally, I'm grateful to God for the miracle of faith, for the grace that covers over my shortcomings, and for the beauty of the world and the cultures in it.

Bryan Bishop has managed research projects for Youth With A Mission (YWAM) for over twenty years. He has taught on communication and mission to audiences in the Americas, Asia, Africa, and Europe. Bryan and his wife, Tamara, live in Colorado Springs, Colorado.